NAKED IN BAGHDAD

NAKED IN BAGHDAD

ANNE GARRELS

WITH LETTERS BY VINT LAWRENCE

FARRAR, STRAUS AND GIROUX

NEW YORK

Farrar, Straus and Giroux
19 Union Square West, New York 10003

Library of Congress Cataloging-in-Publication Data
Garrels, Anne, 1951–
   Naked in Baghdad / Anne Garrels.
      p. cm.
   ISBN 0-374-52903-5 (alk. paper)
   1. Iraq War, 2003—Press coverage.   2. Garrels, Anne, 1951– —Diaries.
   3. Journalists—United States—Diaries.   I. Title.

DS79.76.G373 2003
956.7044′3—dc21

2003056380

Designed by Jonathan D. Lippincott

Maps designed by Jeffrey L. Ward

www.fsgbooks.com

1   3   5   7   9   10   8   6   4   2

TO VINT AND AMER

CONTENTS

INTRODUCTORY NOTE

This is a chronicle of what I saw and heard during my visits to Baghdad, starting with my first assignment in October 2002 before the war, until I left after U.S. troops finally entered the Iraqi capital in April 2003. Some of it is drawn from my reports for National Public Radio; other parts derive from notes and reflections scribbled at the end of long days. It is a personal account of the buildup and conduct of the war, with a foreshadowing of the aftermath that will be with us for a long time to come. Each reporter covering Iraq, whether embedded or non-embedded, had but one window on the conflict and conflicting views. My non-embedded window was from Baghdad.

The book is enriched by e-mails that my husband, Vint Lawrence, sent to family and friends while I was gone. When I was lucky enough to read them I laughed, cried, and loved him all the more for how much he has loved me. As a friend has said, I reported the war and he reported on me, at times with honesty, at times with unbridled affection. Everyone should have such a Boswell.

This is also the story of an extraordinary Iraqi, without whose help I would have been deaf and blind to much that was going on around me. In the presence of "minders," he had the presence of mind to negotiate our way through any manner of obstacles and dangers. Given the continuing uncertainty in Iraq, he has chosen to go by the pseudonym "Amer." I owe him this, and a lot more.

As a radio correspondent, I was not very particular about the spelling of names, which are now to appear in print, so often they are only phonetically, not strictly orthographically, accurate.

May 2003
Norfolk, Connecticut

IRAQ

TURKEY

SYRIA

Mosul•

•Erbil

Kirkuk• Sulaimanlya•

Halabja•

IRAN

Tikrit•

JORDAN

Euphrates River

Baghdad★

Tigris River

Karbala• □ BABYLON

Najaf• **IRAQ** •Amarah

Nasiriya•

Basra•
Umm Qasr•

KUWAIT
Kuwait★ *Persian Gulf*

SAUDI
ARABIA

0 Miles   100   200
0 Kilometers   200

© 2003 Jeffrey L. Ward

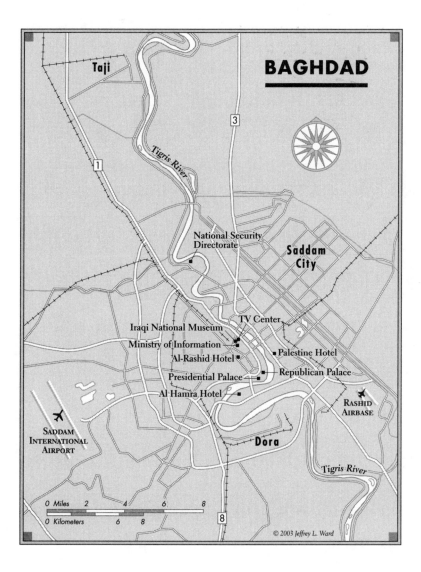

BAGHDAD

Taji

Tigris River

National Security
Directorate

Saddam
City

TV Center

Iraqi National Museum
Ministry of Information
Al-Rashid Hotel

Palestine Hotel

Presidential Palace
Republican Palace

Al Hamra Hotel

RASHID
AIRBASE

SADDAM
INTERNATIONAL
AIRPORT

Dora

Tigris River

0 Miles   2   4   6   8

0 Kilometers   6   8

© 2003 Jeffrey L. Ward

BEFORE

Well hello again,

Just when we were all getting used to the idea that our Annie was going to be more or less gainfully employed organizing the linen closet or darning socks by the fire, the damsel is off again— this time to Iraq. You might be forgiven for thinking that after Afghanistan, Pakistan, and Israel in the last year, NPR could come up with, say, an in-depth series on beach erosion between Bordeaux and Biarritz, but the straws in this outfit all appear to be short.

Remember that intrepid comic book character of our youth, Brenda Starr, who was always getting into and out of impossible scrapes? Well, someone the other day dubbed Annie "Brenda of the Berkshires," a reference to our remote abode up here in the hills of northwest Connecticut. It fits, and it has a certain ring, so I have appropriated it. For those of you who have tolerated my scribblings since 9/11 when she headed off to Tajikistan and points south, these letters will no longer be just Annie Updates but Brenda Bulletins . . .

Brenda, in her packing mode, is curious to observe. Well over a week before she actually leaves, many too many suitcases are dragged out, only to lie opened but untouched for days on the bed in the spare bedroom. Something Zen-like goes on as she circles and stares at the empty cases. Then one morning, in a flurry, there suddenly appears a great pile of brightly colored, neatly folded frocks and form-fitting pants and snappy shirts and fitted jackets— gorgeous oranges, lime greens, bright blues, and pinks predominate. These are the things Brenda would LIKE to take, the things that are in her nature. But inevitably these treasures go back in the closet, replaced by long, loose, formless things that cover everything and button all the way down—the cheerful pile morphs to monotonous blues and blacks. And by the end there are not very many of these, either, because so much technical gear has yet to go in. The old stand-by Sony cassette tape recorder that has been her mainstay all over the world with three dozen cassettes, the new still-unproven mini-recorder that's no bigger than a cigarette box, the satellite phone, the laptop, and an odd assortment of technical gear that makes her pieces sound as if they originated in a nearby mall, not halfway around the world. Stuffed in at the end is a huge wad of unread research, the unfinished expense-accounting from her last trip, a staggering number of pairs of reading glasses, and her one surviving hearing aid, a new one, made by an old Russian friend who is now an audiologist in Jerusalem. This tiny device has fifteen minuscule computers in it instead of four, enabling her to eavesdrop virtually on thoughts. That is, if she remembers to wear it.

Last-minute exotically wrapped cartons of new sophisticated equipment from NPR arrive. Miniature satellite-phone antennae blossom briefly amid the dahlias. An hour before the taxi is due, she is still downloading a complicated NPR program with a cool competence that may keep her safe until she returns.

She left here with a weighty array of journalistic weaponry that is lean, mean, and all business. All but the technical gear was checked-in luggage at JFK, where security pawed through everything; what was neatly packed upon leaving certainly will not be upon arrival. In the end she didn't even carry a change of clothes onto the plane; Brenda, as she will modestly admit, knows—if she knows nothing else—how to SHOP.

So, our Brenda arrived safely in Baghdad from Jordan on Sunday. She spent the three days in Amman waiting for the promised Iraqi visa that never came. It was a quick lesson in how things work over there. She was finally able to reach Ahmed, the Iraqi "fixer" in Baghdad with whom she has been talking for weeks and who had promised to have the visa waiting for her. Ahmed—now follow me on this—said to her, "No problem, all you have to do is contact Nabil in Amman." Well, Nabil wasn't much help but he turned her over to Amjad, who is a fellow big-time fixer in Amman. Amjad told her that he couldn't really help but that Ibrahim could. Ibrahim, in turn, passed her on to Mohammed, who said that for $200 he could set up a breakfast with the Iraqi ambassador. Well, that is how Brenda got her visa. Cheap at the price, it seems, as another news organization had bought the Iraqi ambassador his new car. In the fraying atmosphere of Amman, with everyone squirreling dollars, just about anything is for sale. She also found time in all this to do a yet-to-be-aired piece on how the Jordanians find themselves once again between Iraq and a hard place.

Brenda's claim that she has absolutely no idea how she got her visa strikes some who know her as slightly disingenuous. When her switch is OFF here at home, many make the mistake of assuming that she carries with her overseas that slightly muddled, directionally challenged, technologically inept persona that is so pleasurable and delightful. Don't be fooled. About three weeks ago there was an audible click when the switch went ON. Annie became Brenda in an instant. "Wake me at five" meant wake her at five. Carefully crafted exquisite dinners slid into hamburgers with frozen limas or even "fend for yourself" affairs. Research e-mails poured in. Books were ordered and devoured. The phone was constantly in use to far-flung places at odd hours. Her voice took on a different timbre. Brenda knows very well how to work the system, even if Annie doesn't.

Stay tuned . . .

V

OCTOBER 20, 2002

Vint and I took our usual farewell walk with the dogs just before the taxi came. It was a spectacular autumn day and we talked about all the garden projects we want to do next spring. We talked about everything but Iraq. But when we said good-bye we knew this wasn't just another assignment. If there is to be war, this is the beginning of a long odyssey.

I've never been to Iraq before and have all the fears I always have embarking on any new assignment. I need to hit the ground running, but I need the right people to help me do it.

After finally getting a visa, I arrived in Baghdad from Amman late at night to be met by the 250-pound Ahmed. I've inherited him from other NPR colleagues who have made use of his services in the past. Though he works for an American television network, he moonlights (literally, in this case) for other organizations. His brother is an official with the Information Ministry, so he has the connections necessary to arrange visas, drivers, and hotels—all, needless to say, for hefty fees. He leads me on a mysterious dance through the airport, where endless officials cut in. I try to follow the best I can. Innumerable forms are filled out and stamped with orders not to lose them or I will never get out of the country. What's most important, though, is knowing how to dish out money. The black case containing my satellite phone is sealed with a sticky white label, and I am told very sternly not to open it until I have checked in at the Information Ministry. Given that it's well past midnight, that will have to wait until daylight.

It's an inauspicious beginning. I have just missed probably one of the biggest stories in Iraq in years. While I was traveling, President Saddam Hussein announced a "full, complete, and final amnesty" for tens of thousands of prisoners, opening the doors to Iraq's notorious jails and releasing everyone from pick-pockets to political prisoners into the arms of jubilant crowds.

The decree read throughout the day on Iraqi radio and tele-vision marks the first time Saddam's government has acknowl-edged imprisoning opponents of the regime, despite years of scathing reports from human-rights groups. This appears to be another attempt to rally public support for war with the United States, which looks increasingly inevitable.

As I check into the Al-Rashid Hotel, reporters describe the scene at Abu Ghreib prison, the country's largest. As word of the decree spread, thousands of family members raced to this fortress, which is situated on the outskirts of the city. Chaos broke out. Iraqi officials had announced that five hundred pris-oners would be released every hour, but guards stood by as fami-lies broke through the gates into the prison courtyard to find their loved ones. Prisoners meanwhile pushed their way out. Several were killed in the stampede. As night fell, some family members were still searching in vain for prisoners, calling out for them in the dark or holding up handwritten signs with their names.

The amnesty comes just days after Saddam received a pre-posterous 100-percent approval in a referendum. The govern-ment claimed he got every single vote with every eligible Iraqi participating, and officials say the prisoner release was to thank the people for their support, but the underlying message is clear. In Saddam's Iraq, life, death, and freedom are in the hands of the man who has ruled Iraq since 1979.

The Al-Rashid is full of reporters I know from other assign-ments in other places. Towering over everyone is Nick Turner, a talented cameraman for CBS News. Though he's a little grayer than when we first met, he's as lean and deliciously mean as he was twenty-five-plus years ago, when we were both assigned to

Moscow. He says work conditions are frustrating and will remind me of the former Soviet Union, where raising a camera had the same effect as raising an M16—everyone scattered for cover.

The Al-Rashid Hotel became world famous in 1991, when CNN broadcast from here during the Gulf War. It's a huge complex, and its cavernous halls, full of people I can only assume are intelligence agents, are slightly menacing. By the elevator there is a man whose only job is to watch you get on and off. On the 8th floor, my new home, there's another man monitoring the hallway. His job, I suspect, is also to watch who comes and goes.

It is indeed a familiar setup, developed and perfected in the Soviet Union, where "floor ladies" were also the bane of my existence. When I first arrived in Moscow to be ABC's correspondent in 1979, I lived in the Intourist Hotel for a couple of months while I waited to move into an apartment. Vera Ivanovna was a surly presence whose cleaning was so thorough as to include a regular search of my belongings and the removal of my address book. Though barely over five feet, she also body-blocked anyone trying to visit my room. When I met her again years later, after Mikhail Gorbachev had lifted the veil of fear, she greeted me warmly and apologized for her behavior. "I am so sorry," she said simply. "I always wanted to make you some decent soup because you never ate anything," she recalled, "but I couldn't. You understand."

We exchanged stories about her duties back then, necessary to keep her job, and my efforts to thwart her. We talked about how life had changed for her. While many of her friends were embittered at the loss of Socialist security and scared of an uncertain future, Vera proved to be an indomitable soul. She had had contact with foreigners and an inkling of what life might be like beyond the confines of the Soviet Union. She was enthusiastic about the reforms under way, even though her savings and her pension had evaporated with the crash of the ruble. Too old to benefit from the changes, she nonetheless hoped her children and grandchildren would live a very different life. But in addition to hope, the end of Soviet rule brought chaos and conflict. I have a feeling I am about to watch a repeat.

OCTOBER 21, 2002

I didn't sleep well, nervous about how I'm supposed to tackle this complicated story in a country I don't know. In the cool light of dawn I finally see the famous mosaic on the hotel threshold. In my confusion last night I missed it, but everyone who enters or exits the Al-Rashid must walk over the scowling image of George Bush the elder with the words DOWN WITH USA etched in tile.

Ahmed hands me over to the man who will be my driver. Thirty-eight-year-old Amer is some sort of distant relation. Everyone here seems to be related, but he's the opposite of Ahmed, whose style can only be summed up as "slob." With thick black hair and a perfectly trimmed mustache, Amer is tall, strikingly good-looking, and well-dressed, but most important of all, he has a decent command of English. Ahmed's language skills seem limited to dinars, dollars, and cents.

Amer takes me in tow and we begin another mysterious dance at the Information Ministry. The power to make or break emanates from one small office on the ground floor, where I have been told I will spend as much time sucking up as I will reporting. I pay my obeisances, register my satellite phone, which is duly unsealed, and look for somewhere to work. The prospects aren't good. Work space inside is limited; the few offices are already rented for exorbitant sums, so I find myself camped outside in a dusty courtyard that overlooks a busy, noisy main thoroughfare. Amer helps me scrounge a desk, a rickety chair, and an extension cord to one of the few available electrical outlets.

There is a rigorous system for controlling and monitoring Western journalists in Iraq that has been honed over the years. The Information Ministry's goal is not to facilitate our work, but to make sure we do only what they wish us to. Satellite phones, by which we can communicate, access e-mail, and broadcast to the States, are to be kept in the Information Ministry at all times because officials are leery of these portable machines, which they cannot easily bug. They are nervous about us, and they are nervous that Iraqis could use the phones for uncensored calls. All reporters must also have an officially approved "minder" who will monitor every interview if able. The minders' knowledge of a foreign language is by no means their top skill. A display of loyalty to the regime is. And most Iraqis, familiar with the rules and the penalties for an injudicious remark, are wise enough not to speak to a foreigner even without a minder present. With so many journalists now in Baghdad, minders are in short supply— and it's clear there are a lot of frustrated, unattached reporters milling around the lobby unable to work.

Thanks to Ahmed I hook up with Sa'ad Samarrai, who's reputed to be one of the better minders, whatever that means. Somewhere around fifty, he's suave and his English is superb. He's already working with another journalist, Olivia Ward from Canada. She's naturally not well pleased that I have elbowed in. We "negotiate" the price. In other words, Sa'ad tells me his services will be $100 a day. Little matter that I am already paying the Information Ministry $50 a day for him.

The agenda has already been set. We are going out to water- and sewage-treatment plants to see the ongoing effects of the UN sanctions that were imposed after the '91 Gulf War to exact compliance with UN demands. Crudely put, Iraqi officials blame the sanctions, and the limits on what Iraq can import, for continued health problems. The UN says that if Saddam were to fulfill his obligations the sanctions would be lifted. This trip seems like a good way to get my bearings and see something of Baghdad, and besides, at this point I have no choice. Amer and I get into his black '91 Chevrolet Caprice. Sa'ad and Olivia take a second car.

The streets are packed with traffic. Gas is cheap, but nearly all of the cars are old Chevrolets and Fords with broken windshields. Baghdad is not a charming place. The cement buildings are spare, solid, and utilitarian; there's little vegetation to interrupt the ubiquitous beige and there is virtually nothing left to hint at the city's exotic past, the Baghdad of a thousand years ago, of Ali Baba and the Forty Thieves and other stories from *The Thousand and One Nights*, when the city was the capital of an Islamic empire that stretched from North Africa to the edges of China.

There are no longer any mysterious *souks*. The relics of that world were consumed by floods, sandstorms, and Mongol invaders. Four hundred years of Ottoman rule, ending in 1917, left Iraq one of the most backward and underdeveloped regions of the empire. History seems to have begun with the rise of Saddam and his Baath Party in the '60s, which promised an Arab renaissance, and Saddam's modernization campaign evidently had no tolerance or taste for quaint. But if Baghdad lacks the architectural intrigue of a Cairo, it also doesn't have its teeming masses and widespread poverty. It is well laid out, with good roads. There are hospitals, universities, and shopping centers, vestiges of its recent prosperity. There are imposing government complexes built during the oil boom of the '70s and early '80s, and we pass through sprawling middle-class neighborhoods of respectable two-story houses that give the city the feel of the American Southwest. There are no signs of past U.S. bombing campaigns. The government has repaired almost all the bridges and buildings which were hit in '91 and again in '98. New construction, however, seems to have been limited to the creation of vast presidential palaces and enormous new mosques. Amer points to one mosque, still bristling with cranes and the skeletons of soaring minarets, which he says will be the biggest in the world. He also nods discreetly at several compounds surrounded by crenellated walls: "Saddam's palaces," he says, with barely concealed disgust and no further explanation.

He gives me a quick primer on conditions. The electricity has been largely restored since the '91 Gulf War, despite UN sanctions. Blackouts are less common now. Emergency services such as hospitals are operating without life-threatening power cuts, but as we approach the water-treatment plant he says the deteriorating water system is still a major concern.

Inside the plant, four of eight purification tanks are out of service and a vital sediment filtration machine needs to be replaced. Senior engineer Mohammed Ali Kassim blames the UN sanctions committee for holding up purchase of a new one. The amount of drinking water available to the public is half what it needs. And in rural Iraq the water systems are far worse. Many villages have no access to running water and often depend on brackish wells. All this contributes to endemic gastrointestinal problems and continued high infant-mortality rates.

In the east of Baghdad, in the slum of al-Hansa, barefoot children play in the fetid streets. There's no sewage system. In the boiling summer months water pressure is so low that residents say barely a trickle reaches their houses. They have to illegally cut into the pipes to access water. The runoff from the free-flowing sewage then seeps into the punctured water system. According to my notes, the UN now puts Iraq at 127, the bottom of the list, for overall development. It used to rank 67.

Suddenly there's the sound of music. A ragtag band wends its way through the streets, the drum and trumpet attracting a raucous crowd. Much to Sa'ad's horror, we race after them. They stop outside a one-story house. Sa'ad asks some quick questions, establishes what is going on, and agrees that we can go in. The Sadiq family is sitting in a dark, bare room celebrating the return of their father. He was one of the prisoners released yesterday, and everyone is still clearly in shock. He says he'd expected a life sentence for murdering his cousin even though, under customary law, the family had resolved the problem by paying blood money to the family of the victim. He has nothing but good things to say about Saddam Hussein.

Back in the car, Amer expresses reservations about the prisoner release, given the crime wave that beset Baghdad through much of the 1990s, but he also says many were the victims of an arbitrary system, a poignant statement about the state of Iraqi justice. As we talk, we pass hundreds of people standing silently by the side of the road. "The families of political prisoners," says Amer, a comment he certainly didn't need to offer. They are waiting across the street from the General Security Directorate, one of the most feared buildings in Baghdad. I realize we have just tripped on a much more important story than the prisoner release of yesterday. These are people who are looking for prisoners who did not emerge from the cells, and their silent demonstration is unprecedented.

Amer then gives me a quick lesson on how we are going to work. As long as there are no minders around, he will do what he can "within reason" to help. He warns me to be careful what I say around Sa'ad. When Sa'ad is in the car, I am not to speak to Amer. I am to treat him as nothing more than a dumb driver who follows orders.

Given this opening, I begin to pepper him with questions. He says he started his professional life as a schoolteacher, but when he could no longer afford the luxury of his job he began to work for foreign journalists as a driver. He has three small children. He rents a house in the western part of the city and has no phone. In recent months the government has taken several steps to bind Iraqis to the regime. Rations have been doubled, cars and stipends have been doled out to party loyalists, tribes, and the military. The prisoner release is a good way to make peace with the military, which has suffered purges, and it is also a way to get more fodder for the army. Many of those in prison were draft-dodgers who will now be "persuaded" to join up and stay. The amnesty may also be a gesture to Iraqis living abroad, who have been invited back, but Amer doubts many will respond, since many of those who have come back in the past have been welcomed with arrest or execution.

It was much too dangerous for Amer to stop outside the security complex, where the crowds had gathered. I ask him to leave me at the hotel, telling him I have some work to do for a couple of hours. When he has disappeared, I flag a taxi and return on my own. I wander through the mass of people, mostly women draped in black. Without a translator I can only call out, "Does anyone speak English?" No one will speak directly to me, but as I pass by some whisper without raising their eyes, "My son, gone twelve years," "My husband, eight years," "Where are they? No one will tell us." Within seconds, it seems, the police spot me and hustle me away. I deliberately don't have a tape recorder with me, or a notebook. I try to look as stupid as I can, and they let me leave without further incident.

Back at the Information Ministry we're told there's to be a mass wedding to celebrate Saddam's recent reelection. At a youth club, more than 150 couples gather for a most unromantic union, but the government is picking up the tab and without this help the couples say they could not afford to get married. The brides, so heavily made up and hairsprayed that they look like they're wearing masks, have been provided with long white dresses, veils, shoes, handbags, and gloves. They will be allowed to keep everything but the dresses, which must be returned. Sa'ad is nowhere to be found, and Amer says he cannot translate for me if other minders are present. I find one who speaks one of my known languages—Russian. In fact, it is extraordinary how often Russian is proving to be useful here, as many Iraqis were educated in the former Soviet Union, which had close ties to Saddam's regime through the '80s. The same thing happened in Afghanistan, and while reporting in the West Bank I often resorted to Russian when talking to Palestinian doctors, many of whom were trained by the Soviets. And, of course, in Israel, with the huge immigration of Russian Jews or those passing for Jews, Russian is more useful than Hebrew in many neighborhoods. I certainly never expected to use this language as my main means of communication in so many disparate countries.

OCTOBER 22, 2002

The silent demonstration of yesterday has turned into a protest march to the Information Ministry. Dozens of Iraqis ignore repeated warnings to disperse and gather outside to demand information on the fate of sons and brothers still missing despite the government's decision this week to empty its infamous prisons.

Most are women, swathed in black robes, and most are Shiite Muslims. Though the majority in Iraq, they are underrepresented in a government dominated by Saddam's clan and loyal Sunni Muslim tribes. The Shiites have their origin in a series of disputes within the early Muslim community, starting more than a thousand years ago, over who was the rightful heir to the prophet Mohammed. Differences in doctrine and practice emerged. The Shiites have suffered repeated reprisals at the hands of Saddam's ruling Sunni sect, especially after Shiites in the south rose up against Saddam following the '91 Gulf War and were abandoned to their fate by the United States, which had encouraged them to rebel.

The women beg foreign journalists to help determine the whereabouts of their relatives. One after another tells how a son or husband was picked up, with no explanation, and has not been heard of for years. These women, however, are no fools. They intersperse their whispered pleas with pro-forma praise of Saddam. Careful not to implicate the great leader, they say, "Of course if he knew our relatives were missing he would help. It's his subordinates who are to blame."

Iraqi officials, used to all demonstrations being officially sanctioned, are clearly stunned at the appearance of the crowd, and they are not deceived by the veneer of support for Saddam. No minders will help translate, so I just record every utterance in the hope I can make sense of it later. A CNN reporter who speaks Arabic balks when I ask her to help. She can't afford to be seen assisting me. The authorities see Arabic-speakers among the Western press as a potent threat because they can maneuver without minders. Thugs try to block photographers' cameras. They infiltrate the group shouting pro-government slogans, attempting to turn the demonstration into a full-fledged Saddamfest, but they can't stop the women from getting their plaintive message across. Finally plainclothes security men carrying weapons appear and shove the crowd away. It's not clear if any of the demonstrators have been arrested. In the privacy of the car, Amer later helps translate the tape I have recorded.

Some Western news organizations' representatives have sat inside the Information Ministry, refraining from covering the event, fearing they could jeopardize their Iraqi visas by documenting a so-called "unauthorized demonstration." They were right. Al Jazeera, the Qatar-based satellite channel that broadcasts across the Arab world, had its videotapes confiscated. A

CNN correspondent has been expelled after the network carried the protests live. This is one of the few signs of bravery by CNN, which has curried favor with the Iraqi authorities in order to maintain its substantial presence.

But is maintaining a presence at the cost of not reporting the whole truth worth it? Tonight there was a raging debate among some journalists at the Al-Rashid. One Italian television correspondent told me, "I am here for the big story," meaning the war. Reporters have long played a regrettable game, tacitly agreeing not to report on aspects of Iraq for the sake of a visa. Among the issues that are forbidden: the personalities of Saddam and his sons; the fact that he is widely despised and feared; the terror that his regime has instilled.

CNN and the BBC are seen in real time by Iraqi authorities, who monitor the satellite channels normal Iraqis can't see. This puts a lot of pressure on them to pull their punches and "behave." Myself, I don't see the point in self-censorship. The obvious stories, press conferences, and official statements that are now the fodder for most news organizations can easily be had from outside Iraq. I am here to try to understand how Iraqis see themselves, their government, and the world around them.

OCTOBER 23, 2002

There are many cultural divides here, most obviously between reporters and Iraqis who are scared to speak out. But there are also divisions between the various journalists who have come from around the world, each with his or her own national perspective. Though friendships cross national boundaries, journalists do tend to hang out with their own. There is, however, another divide, and that's between print and television. Their demands are different. The way they cover stories is different. And the means at their disposal are distinctly different. Television folk have much more money, relatively large staffs, and big feet, which means they make a lot of noise wherever they go. They seem to live in another realm. As a mere radio correspondent, I fall somewhere in between print and video, and given that I work for National Public Radio, my feet are small.

While I sit outside in the dusty courtyard, screaming over the sound of traffic down the sat phone to my foreign editor, Loren Jenkins, the networks have comfortable offices with fax machines, round-the-clock access to satellite news, and newswires, not to mention boys who bring glasses of tea. If I sound jealous of certain perks, I am, but I have worked for the networks and have no desire to do so ever again. We were not a good fit. I like being a broadcast reporter, but I revel in the freedom of working alone without a camera crew. I like the intimacy this gives me. People, especially here in a police state, are much more likely to speak openly without a camera shoved in their faces, and because I don't have to match what I write with video, I can weave the story with words and sound, nuance and all. And I am not relegated to only a couple of fleeting minutes. I figure I have the best of all worlds, a blend of broadcast and print.

But tonight I'm feeling sorry for myself. The demands by all the NPR programs are enormous. I'm tired and grubby. I have no idea how I'm going to push this story forward, given how frightened everyone is to talk honestly, even without a camera around. All I can do is create a mosaic and hope that a picture emerges that approximates reality.

I seem to have lucked out with Amer. In every foreign assignment I have ever had, there has always been someone who makes the difference. Every journalist's secret is her driver or "fixer," a local person whose translation skills go well beyond words: Lionya and Irina in Moscow, Mimosa in Kosovo, Wadood and Andar in Afghanistan. These people shared every aspect of their lives so that I could better understand their countries. Working around the clock, in tumultuous and dangerous circumstances, they found the people I needed to see, they got me to the places I needed to get to, and they have become my extended family.

OCTOBER 25, 2002

I am off to collect string. What I want to do and what I can do are two very different things in Saddam's Iraq.

There is growing concern here over a possible war, and it's taking its toll on the country's small private sector. Many Iraqis have stopped purchasing anything but necessities. Private businessmen are watching their modest profits plummet.

Sa'ad takes me to the Nineveh Paint Company, a small family business on the outskirts of Baghdad, which has survived wars, embargoes, and sanctions. I'm foisted on the owner, sixty-one-year-old Bassam Antoon. He has no idea who I am, and I have no idea who he is. We start with basic facts. He has had to cut his staff from twenty to thirteen, but his employees still make far more than government workers, albeit a modest $15 a week. Antoon laughs readily, but his laughter is tinged with hysteria as he faces yet another challenge, the possibility of another U.S. attack. He says he is tired of trying to keep body and soul alive through so many years of uncertainty.

When I ask about his biggest concerns, one of his workers replies, "Ulcers brought on by stress." A devout Muslim, this man indicates he is putting greater and greater faith in God. I am surprised that he doesn't mention Saddam. The economic crisis following Iraq's invasion of Kuwait in 1990 and the subsequent UN sanctions all but shut the paint factory down, but after 1997, when Saddam finally agreed to sell oil under UN supervision, the country began to rebuild. Antoon saw his business pick up, but now it's again in trouble. With the U.S. threat out there, the last thing people are thinking about is repainting their buildings.

Just getting by here takes creativity, and I need to employ some creativity to get Antoon on his own. Sa'ad is getting bored with all the usual questions and Antoon's dutiful, careful answers. I ask to see the factory, and Antoon seizes the opportunity to talk to me alone while Sa'ad is busy on the phone clearing permission for the next round of interviews.

Antoon used to import paint cans. That's simply too expensive now, so he's taken to making his own. An educated man who is proud of what he's achieved, he shows how his workers recycle old oil barrels, turning them into shiny containers for his paint. I turn off the tape recorder, hoping that Antoon will open up a little, and he does. He warns that there could be a backlash if the precarious gains of recent years are destroyed by a U.S. war. He says that young people are frustrated with no jobs, no income, and no way to start lives of their own. He warns that these young people, who have grown up knowing only war and sanctions, feel they have been condemned to isolation by the United States. This, he cautions, will be the generation the West will have to face. While Iraqis blame Saddam for their problems, they also blame the West.

Antoon speaks quickly, looking to see who's listening. It's complicated, he says. He thinks it's much better for the Iraqis to deal with Saddam than for the United States to try to force him out. If left alone, he suggests, Iraqis will get rid of Saddam in as little as a year. Sa'ad appears and the conversation reverts to talk of paint cans.

Iraq's private industrial sector has always been small, but to buy loyalty and to reward cronies Saddam has given the private sector more freedom to operate than in the past. He also uses the private sector to smuggle in goods so that shops can provide Iraqis with at least some of what they need, and at first glance I have to say they seem pretty well stocked. But the right to do business remains under Saddam's control, and he takes his cut.

Next stop—an interview with private businessman Faris al-Hadi, who has a government-approved license to import household appliances. Until the '90s, the government had retained a monopoly. Now, to skirt the sanctions, there are lots of private suppliers, and al-Hadi is one of the most successful.

Al-Hadi readily admits he resorts to smuggling with the full knowledge of the government. He won't discuss the payoffs involved. Just about everything he brings in is outside the purview of the UN sanctions committee, and some items like microwave ovens are banned outright by the UN because someone on the sanctions committee thinks they have a military application. This is a risky business. There's no way to insure illegal shipments, which arrive in leaky vessels from somewhere in the Gulf. One of his boats recently went up in flames and with it $60,000 in videocassettes. With the prospect of a possible war, al-Hadi says he's put all shipments on hold. He's dumping his current stock of television sets at below cost to avoid bigger losses later on, should the United States bomb.

What al-Hadi doesn't say is as revealing as what he does. He does not offer fulsome praise for Saddam or his government, though he does hazard the opinion that weapons of mass destruction are not the key issue for the United States. Oil is, he says firmly, and he believes the United States will press for war regardless of what weapons inspectors might find.

OCTOBER 28, 2002

In his off hours, Amer disappears into the Al-Rashid's Internet café, which piques my curiosity. Inside Iraq there are no cell phones, no instant messaging, and definitely no private e-mail accounts, but, nevertheless, the Internet has finally arrived. After long resisting, Saddam's regime has cautiously allowed Internet access and the window it provides to the rest of the world, and it is now struggling to control the uncontrollable. In the late '80s, the spread of fax machines emboldened and connected student protestors in China, and the fax helped undermine the coup-plotters who eventually tried to overthrow Soviet leader Mikhail Gorbachev. What the flurry of faxes once did in those places, the Internet might do here.

Most in Iraq still get their information the old-fashioned way: in the absence of foreign newspapers and magazines, they search for uncensored news on scratchy broadcasts from the BBC, Radio Monte Carlo, or the Voice of America. When Sa'ad isn't in the car, Amer is continually flipping stations for some "real news." The Iraqis regularly jam VOA's newest Arabic language service, called Radio Sawa, forcing it to jump frequencies and Amer to scan the dial for the latest position, but for a growing number of people, including Amer, the Internet is a growing addiction.

Though it's run by the Iraqi Ministry of Transportation and Communications, the mundane scene in one of the nineteen Internet cafés in Baghdad represents a quiet revolution. Portraits of President Saddam Hussein act as screen-savers, but with the click of a button he disappears and you enter another psychic space.

The regime first permitted Internet access for government ministries a few years ago, but its lack of trust in its people, and the free flow of information, was evident. Back then, even high-ranking officials weren't allowed to send e-mails from their desks. They had to take them to a central clearing office. The first e-mail center for the public opened in early 2000. This year, somewhat amazingly, they added Internet service, and now Iraqi universities are beginning to hook up. Access is so popular, and lines so long, that students are restricted to two hours a week. Recently the government took another major step, permitting some citizens to have Internet connections at home. At a little over $30 a month, this is much too costly for most, but where there are Internet cafés Iraqis can send e-mails and surf the subversive Web for just 50 cents an hour, and most seem happy to pay.

There are limits. The connections are slow because of poor phone lines, and when Iraqis try to access private e-mail boxes such as Yahoo! or Hotmail, they're greeted with a blunt message: ACCESS DENIED. Everything is supposed to go through Uruklink.net, the government-controlled service provider monitored by Saddam's agents. Sometimes, Amer says, it takes quite a while for e-mails to come through, which reinforces suspicions that the government is reading the messages first. Iraqis are cautious about what they say in their messages, and they develop elaborate codes, but Amer describes ways to circumvent restrictions by sending e-mails through other Web sites, and there are talented Iraqi hackers. The Internet is both a blessing and a curse for a sophisticated totalitarian regime for whom information is at once necessary and feared.

Mohammad, a university student, shows me how he can get to just about any news site on this particular night, but he says that if there's aggressive news about Iraq you might find some of the sites suddenly blocked. And porn sites are always inaccessible.

As I look over their shoulders, I can see two students from Saddam University looking for information on lasers. They glance at me nervously, since lasers are such a sensitive subject for those trying to impede Iraq's weapons programs. I suspect they don't want me to see what they are accessing. They quickly point out that, while a lot of information is available for free on the Internet, they can often access only abstracts. To get an entire article they have to pay, but because of sanctions they don't have credit cards. Money, they say, is the problem.

Amer says he regularly uses the Internet to communicate with an Austrian company for whom he's become the local rep. He is helping them bid on contracts for water-treatment plants. Now I know what all those folders are in the trunk of his car. He says we will be able to communicate by e-mail when I'm outside Iraq, but once again he warns me to be careful about what I say or write.

A code has already developed between us. It started when we were passing the zoo. Amer mentioned that Saddam's elder son Uday has a passion for tigers, walking down the street with them like some might walk their dogs. "Tigers" is now our password for Saddam and his circle. We have begun to trust each other in a society where no one trusts anyone. It's a gamble we both seem to be taking.

I've barely arrived, but it's already time to apply for the dreaded visa extension. Journalists come into the country with visas that last only ten days, giving the Information Ministry firm control over its flock. By now I've been let into the secrets of bribes, sycophancy, and groveling. Some reporters submit copies of their stories to show how friendly they are. Others buy officials expensive gifts. Some order lunch or dinner to be delivered to officials in their offices. I have given one ministry official a nice tie, but I have so far failed to make any impression at all on the super-keeper, Uday al-Tae. He is the director general of the Information Ministry and the man who ultimately decides our fate. He is in his early fifties and once worked at the Iraqi embassy in Paris, where he reportedly ran a network of Iraqi agents in Western Europe. Eventually he was expelled from France, but he still loves to show off his French, and he has an eye for French women that hasn't done me one bit of good. He is cutting back on the number of journalists currently in Baghdad, and it doesn't look like I'll be staying on. NPR, for better or worse, is not on his radar screen.

OCTOBER 31, 2002

President Bush used a campaign swing through South Dakota today to issue another in what have become almost daily warnings to the United Nations: "Do the right thing," he said, "and force Iraq to disarm now." He warned that if the UN won't act and if Saddam Hussein won't disarm, the United States will lead a coalition of nations to disarm him.

Iraqis say they hope their government will readmit the UN inspectors to avoid a military confrontation, but they also ask why the United States is pressing this issue now. And people in Baghdad seem gripped not by the uncertain future, about which they can do little, but by nostalgia for a great proud past which gave rise to the legends of *The Thousand and One Nights*.

I drop in on an elderly barber on Al-Rashid Street, the heart of what passes for old Baghdad. If the Americans bomb this area, Ikmat al-Hella says, they will take away the city's memory. He's a tiny man who sports a frayed shirt, ancient pinstriped trousers, and suspenders. He speaks a little English, and a friend of his speaks a little more. At seventy-nine he's too old to be frightened. He recalls Baghdad in the '30s and '40s when it was little more than a small town. He regales me with reminiscences of the British occupation and Iraq's brief fling with a monarchy, when he used to clip the beard of King Faisal until Faisal was killed in a military coup in 1958. Ikmat talks about the golden age of the '70s, when newfound oil wealth propelled Iraq into the forefront of the Arab world and he would dance until dawn in the city's nightclubs and risqué cabarets. He's hardly the picture of a lady-killer, but you wouldn't know that listening to his tales. A monarchist at heart, he says, "Revolution, revolution after revolution have brought us to destruction."

Many of Iraq's best and brightest have fled the country. It's estimated that three to four million now live overseas, not an insignificant proportion of a population that is somewhere about 25 million. Once out of the country, they suffer the fate of so many exiles in so many other countries. They are dismissed at home by those who have had to stay and suffer. When I ask around about the exiled politicians and groups the United States is trying to back, Iraqis show little interest and even less support.

After my solitary walk, I hook up with Sa'ad to go to nearby Babylon, once the site of the Hanging Gardens, one of the eight wonders of the ancient world. It is now an archaeological travesty. It's been reconstructed to look like a theme park. There are, however, still some raw ruins nearby where laborers continue to excavate Iraq's glorious past for a mere $3 a month. One of Saddam's many new palaces looms in the background. It's forbidden to take a tourist snap of the site if the palace is in the frame, which pretty much eliminates all photography. Even with Sa'ad in attendance, or because of Sa'ad, an archaeologist refuses to speak. He is embarrassed and comes up later to apologize. He speaks good English and says, "It's just better to be silent." All in all, the trip is pretty much a bust.

Later, in a smoky Baghdad teahouse, patrons throw dice on backgammon boards. "War," they say nonchalantly, "we're used to it." A combination of bravado and resignation is easily found here, but a couple of men take advantage of Sa'ad's momentary absence to convey through furtive glances and knowing looks that they are eager for change. One man says, "It's oil that got us into all this trouble." He says oil is driving U.S. policy. "Oil is our blessing and our curse." Despite being an American, I am warmly welcomed, with one old fellow grinning and saying, "I'm lucky to meet you," as he tosses the dice.

A retired schoolteacher suggests that President Bush is making the situation worse for Iraqis by threatening to invade. "U.S. pressure is merely uniting the country and making Saddam more popular among the people," he says. This seemingly safe comment is accompanied by a shake of the head as if to add, "Don't you get it?"

In my constant search for string with which to weave some kind of story, we head out to the English Language Department at Baghdad's Mustansariyeh University, where I fall into conversation with a charming forty-one-year-old man. A jeweller, with a passion for learning English, he's attending night classes. He hints at a wasted life and unfulfilled dreams. He spent ten years at the front, first during the Iran-Iraq war, and then in Kuwait. He was captured by the Americans, who, he says, treated him very well—a treasonous remark. He says he never married because of the wars. Now, by studying English, he's hoping to rebuild a shattered life. He wants to travel abroad but dares not say where. "Please don't embarrass me," he says as I push the issue, "please don't embarrass me." In other words, don't get me into trouble by making me say more than I already have said.

The surreal nature of conversations here, monitored or otherwise, becomes painfully clear at the Iraqi Women's Federation. I am trying to get at what has happened to Iraq's middle class. Many middle-class women come here for computer training so they can help supplement their families' dwindling income. One woman, who is loath to give her name, says she is learning Excel because "Life is too hard, too hard." I ask what her husband does, and she answers, "Oh, what he can." Later Sa'ad confesses he knows this woman very well. Her husband is one of the prisoners Saddam recently released. He had been held for eight years, accused of spying for Germany. "Doing what you can" suddenly takes on a different meaning.

BRENDA BULLETIN: OCTOBER 31, 2002

Dear All,

Twenty or so years ago a writer/journalist's friend spent a number of weeks with me here in Norfolk. During the day, we laconically collaborated on a book, *The Seven Deadly Sins Today*. I tried to put pictures to his eloquent if idiosyncratic update of "The Big Seven." Henry claimed intimacy with several—Pride, Anger, and Lust. Gluttony for him was more or less confined to alcohol. Envy and Avarice he tasted only fleetingly. Sloth was anathema. My box score on the subject remains classified. At night, when work was done for the day, the bottle of Scotch would come out and the talk would begin.

What Brenda is going through in Iraq at the moment brought back one particular conversation Henry and I had very late one night all those years ago. Most journalists, he maintained—and he could be harsh on his own profession—are little more than collectors of beads. They go through life searching for the gaudiest, the sexiest, the most colorful beads they can find without much thought as to how they relate to one another. They sweep them up, pop them in their sack, and move on. Good journalists, on the other hand, he insisted, have a string of a story onto which they thread the beads they choose. And the choice of any new bead must expand upon or inform the beads already on the string. So the choice may not be the most eye-catching bauble but one that connects and fits and fills out. Getting the string thing right is hard enough; finding that elusive illuminating bead can be even more difficult.

Brenda has two strings working; the effects of the embargo on the Iraqi population and the mad despotism of Saddam. To get to the first, she has to go through the second. The beads she finds are so encrusted with thirty years of suspicion and oppression that she never quite knows what she has found. It is maddening work.

V

NOVEMBER 1, 2002

Amer is late arriving at the hotel. His car was sideswiped by a government official's car. Though it was the official's fault, he can do nothing. He is furious at his impotence. "I know my rights," he spits out sarcastically. Sa'ad appears, cutting short his invectives. He's wearing a garish but very expensive plaid wool-and-silk sports jacket with a perfectly matched sportshirt. I can't help but think I am paying for all this.

Today's program starts with a return visit to a woman who had struck my fancy during an earlier interview. Forty-one-year-old Huda al-Neamy is a professor of political science, one of many educated middle-class Iraqis struggling to maintain dignity and a semblance of past prosperity on a salary of $15 dollars a month.

I had first seen Huda in her office but was anxious to fill out the portrait by visiting her at home, which in today's Iraq is not always easy. Luckily, she agreed. The tiles in the living-room floor have buckled, but there's no money for repairs. Her husband, a former army officer, has left the military, where he could no longer make a decent living, to open up a small convenience store. As she lights up one cigarette after another, Huda says she's weary of a situation from which she sees no exit. She yearns for a normal life that has eluded her for twenty years. But while she cautiously suggests that Iraq may have made mistakes by launching wars against its neighbors she says the U.S. treatment of the Iraqis is unjustified.

While Israel is allowed to flout UN resolutions, she says, Iraq is not. And the Bush administration's failure to threaten tough actions against North Korea for its nuclear-weapons program reinforces her belief that the real American objectives in Iraq are oil, support for Israel, and domination of the region. The thought of a war in which Iraq could be dismembered or dissolve into ethnic and religious conflicts makes her shudder. She warns that "it would be a terrible mistake."

In honor of Palestinians and their unfulfilled aspirations, she named her third and last child Quds, which means "Jerusalem" in Arabic. Now eleven, Quds says she identifies with Palestinian children who, she says, are suffering unjustly just as she is.

Like many in the Iraqi middle class, Huda grew up in a secular atmosphere, but Islam has come to play a much more important role here in recent years, a result, she explains, of despair. The government has encouraged and reflected this shift toward religion, justifying its rule on Iraqi patriotism, defense of Palestine, and Islamic solidarity. It was only ten years ago, when she was in her thirties, that Huda began to wear a head scarf. But while she has sought refuge in religion, she is quick to say this should not be mistaken for fundamentalism. "I am from an educated family," she says. "I respect all human beings."

We disappear into the kitchen, away from Sa'ad, who once again seems bored with the proceedings. As she prepares Turkish-style coffee, a thick strong brew, conversation turns to girl talk. She pulls off her head scarf. She laughs that a scarf, a sign of devotion, also has its practical aspects. Her blondish-red hair is in need of a dye job that costs money she doesn't have. Her daughter, a serious child, chides Huda to cover her hair completely. I can see that, proud as she is of her daughter's anger at Israel and concern for Palestinians, Huda is uncomfortable with the degree to which Quds has taken to her religion. This attractive, vivacious woman rearranges the scarf her own way, trying out various styles for me. She pointedly leaves some strands of hair visible, flouting strict religious convention.

She too has a nostalgia for the golden age of the '70s, when oil wealth dramatically improved people's lives and Iraq appeared to be joining the rest of the world, but then came the '80s and the Iran-Iraq war. Money grew tight even before the UN punished Iraq for its invasion of Kuwait in 1990. Huda once traveled to Europe. She dreamt of studying in the United States, but she can't afford any of that now. And anyway, she points out sadly, it's unlikely that a Western country would give her, an Iraqi, a visa,

She wants her children to see many civilizations, different people, different cultures, so that they can learn to respect others. For now, though, this family is mired in its isolation and growing bitterness at a world that has rejected them.

It's at moments like this that I revel in being a female reporter, which on balance has been a distinct advantage. Men generally deal with me as a sexless professional, while women open up in ways that they would not with a man. Hard as it was to break into journalism back in the dark '70s, and with few role models out there to follow, I have only benefited from my sex, reporting from overseas especially, ironically in societies where women are sequestered. Whether in Afghanistan or Saudi Arabia, I can walk both sides of the street, talking the talk with male officials while visiting the women's inner sanctums, which are often off-limits to foreign males. And being an older woman has its advantages too. I would never have been able to interview a mullah along the Pakistan-Afghan border were he not assured in advance that I was an "old woman." He had tutored the young American muslim John Walker Lindh, who then went to fight for the Taliban until he was captured by U.S. forces. However, I apparently did not look as old as the mullah had anticipated, and on my arrival his aides demanded I wear a *burka* for the entire interview because "he had the natural feelings of a man," which he apparently could not control. Enveloped in the burka's stifling blue nylon pleats and peering through a square of mesh while trying to push buttons on the tape recorder and take notes was not pleasant, but it certainly wasn't impossible.

As for covering wars, the dangers are basically the same whether you are male or female. Bullets don't discriminate, and while some of my bosses in the past have expressed concerns about the risk of rape, my response has been that men can be tortured just as badly, if in different ways.

At the hotel tonight I spot a group of prostitutes, imported from Russia. According to Amer, they are here to service Saddam's elder son Uday and his friends. They are scantily dressed and cause quite a stir with some of the male reporters, who would be well advised to stay clear. Bored with their assignment, these young women perform an erotic dance out in the hotel gardens. I wander out to talk to them. They are delighted to chatter in Russian, but a security guard comes up and cuts off the conversation before I am able to find out more about their backgrounds or collect any juicy tidbits.

NOVEMBER 2, 2002

A visit to Saddam City, the part of Baghdad where more than two million of Iraq's Shiites live, has been nixed, so instead we head for al-Adhamiya, a middle-class neighborhood and bastion of Baathist support. The girls school we are taken to seems pretty well appointed. The students in their navy-and-white uniforms primp and giggle as they prepare to have their senior photograph taken. But when a microphone appears, they miraculously refer to notes tucked in their pinafores on why America should not invade Iraq. They spout well-rehearsed answers regardless of the question. Asked if they might have been advised about our arrival in advance, the girls respond vehemently with "No," but they aren't very good at lying and the truth quickly emerges. Once they have performed their assigned declarations, they can't hide their curiosity about how girls their age live in America. They want to know how I have a family and do the job I do, a question I am hard-pressed to answer. Seventeen-year-old Noor, one of but a few who is not wearing a headscarf, pipes up, "I want to be a lawyer," and adds, "I think the most important priority now for women in society is to take part and get what we wish. Only second is marriage."

Saddam's secular revolution gave women in Iraq a remarkable degree of freedom compared to others in the rest of the Arab world. Despite the continued constraints of tradition, they prided themselves on their education, but Saddam's spending on wars, the subsequent sanctions, demographics, and the shift to a more conservative religious atmosphere are cramping their style. Overall literacy rates, which reached an impressive 87 percent by 1985, began to plummet as Saddam expended billions on the Iran-Iraq war. Following the imposition of UN sanctions in 1991, only 45 percent of girls can now read. Twenty-three percent of Iraqi children of primary-school age are not enrolled in school now, with twice as many girls dropping out as boys. There is the specter of a lost generation, with girls taking the bigger hit.

These girls are among the fortunate ones, and when the subject turns to their future professions they shout out "engineer," "doctor," or "teacher," but even here the headmistress says she is struggling to stem a soaring dropout rate. With so many men killed during recent wars or going abroad to make a living, girls are under pressure to marry early or risk finding no spouse at all. Given that more and more families are in economic distress, the school tries to raise money among the wealthier parents to help keep those in need from quitting.

The discussion is veering in too many directions for Sa'ad's peace of mind. The effect of UN sanctions is the accepted topic, and he tries to keep questions and answers in that box. Headmistress Selwa al-Sharbati obliges and pulls out a photograph. "This is my big sister," she says. "She was also a headmistress, but she died of breast cancer because of the UN sanctions." The UN has not permitted the importation of spare parts, let alone new radiation machines, because they might be diverted for military uses.

Later on at a Baghdad hospital, Dr. Saad Medi Hasani links Iraq's high infant-mortality rates to both sanctions and the crisis in education. He says illiterate mothers don't know what is harmful and what isn't. He says they don't know about vaccines. As we stand talking in one of the wards, a woman from a nearby village, one of the poor Shiite majority, cuddles her child. She is draped in black. Her face has smeared blue markings on it—tribal tattoos. She doesn't know her age but guesses she's about twenty-two. Dr. Hasani translates, saying she never went to school. She can't read or write, and she doesn't plan to send her children to school.

Her youngest, a one-year-old son, suffers from parasites transmitted by dogs and sand flies. Dr. Hasani says this could have been avoided by using repellent or sleeping nets, but that the family had neither the knowledge nor the money. Now he says there's no hope. He says the only treatment is a drug called Pentostan, another one of the items on the UN proscribed list. This woman doesn't have the money to find it on the black market. Her child is going to die.

NOVEMBER 3, 2002

As anticipated, there's no visa renewal. I go through the departure ritual, which requires paying the hotel with shopping bags full of Iraqi dinars and forking out vast sums of dollars in accumulated fees to the Information Ministry. The serial number of each bill must be listed, presumably to ensure the money is not stolen before it reaches Uday's office. The process takes hours, and is not made any faster by the cashier, who lost most of his fingers in the Gulf War. Then there are the necessary letters and stamps to confirm that I am not skipping the country without settling my accounts. The last step is taking in my satellite phone so that it can be sealed and documented, lest I leave it behind for some Iraqi to have fun with.

I leave Mr. Mohsen $100, a modest contribution, but I hope he will look favorably on my next visa application. The Information Ministry wants to clear the decks for the moment. The staff is exhausted from monitoring us. I am exhausted from being monitored. As the milling horde waits outside his office to demand visa extensions, Mohsen is relieved that I have chosen to go without a fight. He closes my expanding file, saying, "You are very well behaved." Little does he know, but may he believe it.

BRENDA BULLETIN: NOVEMBER 4, 2002

Brenda, ever mindful of her local civic responsibilities, landed in New York late today from Amman in time to vote here on Tuesday. She is on her way to Norfolk as I finish this.

"Surreal, difficult, and expensive" best describes the past two weeks. She will tell you that working in Baghdad was as difficult as anything that she has ever done. Everywhere Brenda went, her government minder was sure to go—making her job all but impossible.

Pleasant enough in person, her constant shadow cast a pall on virtually every conversation. Occasionally, she would slip the leash, but even when on her own the most that she could get out of the people was that they were tired of war, tired of the struggle to retrieve a modicum of what they had before the Gulf War, and fearful that they would lose it all over again. By language unspoken, some made clear that they were also tired of Saddam. But U.S. threats had solidified popular support for him. Did you know that in Iraqi Arabic "BUSH" means "empty" or "nothing"?

The only bit of levity came after a long, hot marginal morning of interviews when her minder and Brenda had the following colloquy:

Annie, why are you so thin? You don't eat. Don't you ever get hungry?

Not when I'm working.

Oh, some people have to eat sometimes.

Does that mean that you want to get something to eat?

Oh, that is a very good idea.

So between constantly buying everyone food, paying exorbitantly for her minder and driver, shelling out daily to the Ministry of Information just for the privilege of being there, and paying for her dingy but pricey hotel room, it was an expensive two weeks. Oh yes, and then there were the hundreds of dollars in bribes that Brenda had to pay at the airport just to get out of the country. Once in Amman and looking back, Brenda was unsure, all in all, if it had been worth it. It was, for one of Brenda's redeeming virtues is that she has never quite figured out how good she is. Ah, I think I hear the taxi.

Ta-ta,

V

BRENDA BULLETIN: DECEMBER 1, 2002

Brenda spent the past couple of weeks getting some sleep, reveling in the domesticity foreign travel denies her, and packing up again. She was also, once again, constantly on the phone at strange hours coaxing a visa out of unenthusiastic Iraqi officials.

We spent a last glorious four days in Vienna with my daughter Rebecca, who lovingly calls our girl "Wism," as in wicked stepmother. And then she headed more or less east, and I west. However, the only route to Baghdad from Austria proved to be a most circuitous one. At 8 p.m. she flew Czech Air to Prague; from there she caught a flight to Beirut that landed at 2 a.m.; four hours later she was on a flight to Amman and then, after collecting her hard-won visa, she caught the 9 p.m. flight into Baghdad.

To while away the down-time of the cat-and-mouse game that is so much of her life these days, Brenda has taken up a new indoor sport: embroidery. Madame Dufarge incarnate, Brenda cross-stitches away, artfully recording the elusive sites of Weapons of Mass Destruction on pillowcases collected from the better hotels en route.

The question has arisen as to why the good lady heads for the farthest, most Godforsaken parts of the globe on such a frequent basis. I have chosen to ignore the opinion most often voiced: that it has something to do with me, the five dogs, the two cats, and my large and overbearing family. A second explanation is more palatable. Those who are familiar with her own family have perhaps picked up on certain manifest patterns of obsessive-compulsive behavior. As noted previously, a gear gets thrown and this otherwise delightful, ofttimes wafty lass becomes steely-eyed, focused, intrepidly brave, and dogged. Nothing, not even me, five dogs, two cats, and my large and overbearing family can stand in her way. And then there is a third possibility, the one I like best. She was simply unable to get everything that was on her Christmas list when she was last there, and well, pashmina by any other name is just wool from Land's End.

Cheers,

V

DECEMBER 3, 2002

It looks like the bribe to Mohsen and dozens of subsequent phone calls worked. A visa was waiting at the Iraqi embassy in Amman. Ahmed was at the airport in Baghdad to meet me. He says Sa'ad is again my minder but Amer can't work for me as his longtime Japanese clients have arrived. He has a contract with them and there's nothing I can do. I am desolate.

We do the now-familiar dance through the airport. The "fees," however, have increased, perhaps because people know that time is running out and they want to make as much money now as they can. And just when it looks like we have sailed through, there's a hitch. I have to get a letter from the Information Ministry before customs will release my satellite phone. This requires a trip back to the airport.

I race to the Information Ministry to get the necessary documents before officials pack up for the night, and then I head back to the airport. With hope flouting reality it was built after the '91 Gulf War, but given the continued UN sanctions there aren't many flights into Baghdad, and by the time I return the airport is deserted. The guards demand money before they will let me in. I wander around the sepulchral halls and finally track down the lone official who's waited because of the promise of a meal, which the driver and I bought for him along the way. He hands over the sat phone, and I go back to the Information Ministry, where it is registered and unsealed. This time, though, I am not going to be able to work here. My "office space" out in the courtyard has been turned into a construction site. For reasons that defy understanding, the Information Ministry is expanding the building. These guys are living in never-never land. The new offices won't be finished before there's a war, when this entire building undoubtedly will be turned to ash. And if there isn't a war, the number of journalists will drop off dramatically and there will be no one to rent the new offices.

I decide to risk it and take the satellite phone to the Al-Rashid. When I check in, I ask for a room with a view over the swimming pool, the best direction for locking on to a satellite. For yet more money, reception is happy to oblige.

DECEMBER 4, 2002

The smarmy Uday al-Tae is still the managing director at the Information Ministry, but the simian Mohsen has been eclipsed by a new man who's been put over him to run day-to-day operations. Qadm al-Tae (a distant relation to his boss, Uday) is definitely in a different class: organized and refreshingly straightforward. Nonetheless this means ingratiating myself with yet another official. The ten-day-visa rule still holds, and within seconds of my arrival it's clear that reporters remain obsessed with the issue of visa extensions. Who gets them and how is a subject of endless speculation and jealousy. And there's a notice announcing a hike in the daily fees we have to pay for the pleasure of being in Iraq. They have doubled to at least $200 per person per day. Television companies pay far more.

Sa'ad now has five journalists in tow, from each of whom he continues to demand and receive $100 a day. With the shortage of minders, let alone those who speak English, he can call the shots. A lot of reporters still have no one to work with and are more or less stuck in the Information Ministry with access only to official press conferences.

The story this time round is going to be inspections. Saddam Hussein has agreed to UN resolution 1441 demanding the return of UN inspectors after a four-year break. So far, the Iraqi government has been surprisingly compliant, a strategy that could prove more vexing to the Bush administration than Saddam's usual defiance. But the new UN resolution also stipulates inspections of presidential palaces as well as interviews with Iraqi scientists without Iraqi officials present, either inside the country or outside if need be. These are potential flashpoints, but analysts and diplomats I've spoken to wonder whether the United States has underestimated Iraq's capacity to cooperate, since the regime's very survival is at stake.

At the Al-Rashid tonight, I hear a voice bellowing, "Bella!" across the lobby. It can only be one person, Lorenzo Cremonesi from Italy's *Corriere della Sera*. His short blond hair stands straight up on end as usual. His eyes sparkle with devilish merriment. In an obscenely revealing pair of running shorts, he's obviously just come back from a ferocious bout of physical exercise, his everyday way of dealing with tension. It's great to see him even though he immediately yanks the cigarette out of my hand and, as ever, chastises me for smoking.

We met in Afghanistan last year not long after four journalists were killed there. One of them was Maria Grazia Cutuli, his colleague at the *Corriere*, and Lorenzo had been sent to Afghanistan to investigate her death. It's hard to believe that only a year has passed since then. With the situation in Afghanistan still far from settled, who would have guessed we would meet again in Baghdad with another U.S. intervention in the offing?

It really was almost exactly a year ago, following the "rout" of the Taliban. After months reporting from the north of Afghan-istan in the run-up to the fall of Kabul, I had taken a break and was trying to get in again from Pakistan. The border was sud-denly closed without explanation. What I didn't know was that a caravan of my peers had been attacked a few hours down the road inside Afghanistan.

When I finally drove into Jalalabad the next day, I found out the details. A convoy of journalists had left Jalalabad for Kabul. Suddenly thieves stopped the second and third cars near the vil-lage of Sarobi. They pulled out four journalists. Within minutes all were dead, shot in the back, their bodies left near the road. The rest of the convoy fled back to Jalalabad, where I found them in shock.

It was soon Thanksgiving. The American journalists orga-nized a dinner inviting everyone, regardless of nationality, who was at the Spin Ghar Hotel. Turkeys had been located, dis-patched, and stuffed. Collecting ingredients in the market had been a challenge, but this traditional meal had taken on a new meaning, in addition to providing some sanity in the midst of madness. Everybody was too frightened to move out of Jalalabad. A somber group gathered around several tables laid end to end. Pam Constable of *The Washington Post* had been in the deadly convoy, and she raised a glass to her friends who had not sur-vived it. Many of us hadn't known the four journalists who were killed, but we knew what they were doing, and why they were in Afghanistan, and no one could help but think, "There but for the grace of God go I." In "dry" Afghanistan, there was only one bottle of wine for the assembled group, numbering over forty, and as it was passed down the table everyone was chided to take but a sip. I could only think it was like Holy Communion, which I had not attended in years.

Geraldo Rivera, who's recast himself as a war correspondent, arrived as the meal was under way. He seated himself at the end of the table, as if this were the way we always dined. He was catered to by an obsequious entourage. He was also surrounded by a contingent of armed guards he had hired. He had not yet announced that he, too, was packing heat, and ready to take on Osama bin Laden *mano a mano*, but it was clear he was playing by different rules that blurred the lines between journalist and combatant. He was upping the ante and I didn't want to be in his playpen.

The next day I decided I would go on to Kabul alone, with a trusted translator. Some journalists wanted to mount another convoy, but I was not anxious to travel in a large group, especially if weapons were involved. Journalists weren't using public transportation. This seemed like a window of opportunity. Bus drivers told us they had not been attacked. They were willing to take us, so I decided to go for it. I didn't tell anyone in the hotel about my plans because I was nervous about the Afghans who were hanging around the lobby. It was impossible to know who they were and where their sympathies lay. At five in the morning, my translator and I boarded the bus. Wrapped in a shawl, I tried to appear as inconspicuous as possible. Along the way, Afghan passengers pointed out the turn in the road where the four journalists had been killed. That day there was nothing to suggest that the particular rocky curve was different from any other. Had I not known what had happened I would have thought it merely a starkly beautiful landscape. The trip was uneventful and we arrived safely in Kabul.

DECEMBER 5, 2002

The Bush administration continues to insist that Iraq has weapons of mass destruction. The Iraqis insist that they don't.

UN weapons inspectors say they are satisfied with progress and will speed up the pace in the weeks ahead.

Our daily routine for now is to track the inspectors. In the early morning fog, a phalanx of UN vehicles speeds out of the Canal Hotel, which is the inspectors' base, for what's become the daily chase through the streets of Baghdad and beyond. First, the UN's white four-wheel-drive Toyota Land Cruisers head west, then north, then west again, all to keep the Iraqis and us in suspense about their ultimate destination. Today, after a two-hour circuitous drive, they eventually reach al-Muthanna, where gates immediately open. Chief Weapons Inspector Demetrius Perricos quips that he is going to the moon, and it's hard to argue with his description. With the exception of the weapons factory, the bleak desert landscape stretches as far as the eye can see. Inspectors in blue baseball caps spend five hours scouring the spread-out installation that was once the heart of Iraq's chemical- and biological-weapons industry. It was largely dismantled during earlier inspections in 1998, and later, when we are permitted to enter, I see the carcasses of disabled equipment, each tagged with one of the inspectors' four-year-old labels.

As we wait outside, dozens of camels wander by, a weird contrast to the sophisticated weapons Iraq had or still has. I finally see Amer, who's back working with his Japanese. He hasn't gotten my e-mails because the Iraqi government has temporarily suspended Internet service, since the United States has been flooding the country with messages urging Iraqis not to fight in the event of war. He has brought me some food, which I happily gobble up, but my new driver is jealous. Given how vicious the backbiting can be, Amer says he has to keep his distance. Ahmed is jealous because I clearly like Amer more than I like him, and he undoubtedly fears that he could lose his lucrative commissions. In addition to the money I have shelled out for visa support, he gets a hefty chunk of the $100 I ostensibly pay the driver each day. Amer would do a much better job, but he doesn't have the protection of close relatives in the Information Ministry and can't risk moving into Ahmed's territory.

The crunch comes this weekend. Iraq has until Sunday to provide a detailed list of its biological, chemical, nuclear, and missile programs. Today Baghdad once again denied having weapons of mass destruction, which puts it on a direct collision course with the United States. Washington insists it knows Iraq has them and demands full and frank disclosure, warning it will disarm Iraq, by force if necessary. Iraq promises to provide a huge amount of material on its arms programs, but it says those programs include only activities that are allowed.

With late-night press conferences and late-night deadlines, I've been living on room service, but tonight I decide to break out of my enforced isolation and try the "National Restaurant" downstairs. It's always empty, but the menu seems more enticing than the grim coffee shop down the hall where the rest of the international press corps hangs out. The manager is clearly delighted to have a customer. With no one around, he starts talking remarkably freely. His name is Faez. He's a Christian, a minority in Iraq. He prepares a delicious meal of hommous and grilled lamb, followed by succulent dates, for which Iraq was once famous. He tells me that dates are Iraq's version of Viagra, and packs up a box for me to take home. He also offers me some red wine, which is far more useful just at the moment. It appears in a discreet tumbler with a can of Pepsi placed next to it for camouflage. Under Saddam's current rules, bars have been closed down and booze is only to be imbibed at home. Faez dismisses the waiters, anxious to talk about the situation in relative privacy. He asks what I think will happen. He is evidently of two minds about a war and the removal of Saddam. He makes it clear that he hates the regime, but he is scared to death that what might follow could be even worse.

DECEMBER 6, 2002

Inspections of Iraqi military sites have been suspended for two days while Muslims celebrate the end of the fasting month of Ramadan. At Baghdad's main amusement park, there are screams of happiness and excitement as the rusty roller-coaster dives down the track. For a brief moment, families here appear to have shed whatever fears they might harbor. Most are from Saddam City, a poor Baghdad neighborhood hit hard by sanctions, and are scraping by on tiny salaries and government food handouts. But today they are decked out in new clothes. Women wear their wedding jewelry, or what's left of it. Most have had to sell off anything of value to feed and clothe their families. A thirty-two-year-old government worker who makes a mere $10 a month is splurging on his nieces and nephews. He's brought them to play video games. "Today," he declares, "there is no thought of war."

A photographer, Nadeen Juhad Akadi, says business has never been better. As he snaps families in their holiday finery, he says people are optimistic that the embargo will be lifted soon because if the inspectors do their job successfully they will find Iraq has no illegal weapons.

He echoes the words of President Saddam Hussein that people must be patient. They must let the inspectors disprove U.S. allegations that Iraq continues to have weapons of mass destruction. Despite the threat of war coming out of Washington, Iraqis smile and ask to have their photograph taken with me. Sa'ad, my minder, is in constant attendance, so I'm left to wonder what people really think.

Next to the amusement park is one of Baghdad's many monumental war memorials. It's customary on Eid, the holiday celebrating the end of Ramadan, to honor the dead. Children race around playing tag, seemingly oblivious to the toll Iraq's recent adventures have taken. This memorial, which resembles a vast blue teardrop, commemorates the Iran-Iraq war that ran for eight years in the '80s. The names of 500,000 Iraqis who were killed are inscribed on the walls. A man whispers in English that in fact far more died in the war. He does not answer when I ask if Saddam's policies are worth such suffering.

The dark museum, housed below-ground, is moving in its unusual simplicity. Instead of Baathist bombast there are modest glass cases showing the personal effects of soldiers who were killed: cigarettes and lighters, ID cards and half-finished letters to family members. I ask Sa'ad to translate one of the letters. It's from a wife to her husband. It was found in the soldier's pocket after he was killed. "I am very longing to see you and your smile, my dear," Sa'ad begins. He breaks off and turns away. His face is damp with tears. He's embarrassed, recovers, and refuses to discuss his feelings.

On the return trip from the amusement park I'm alone in the car with the driver. In central Baghdad we pass one of Saddam's many extravagant palaces, an obscene expression of his aspirations to grandeur. I point to it and ask him what it is. He blanches, warning it's not wise to look too closely and that it is dangerous to stop here. With no encouragement he then goes on to say that Saddam has no interest in or understanding of a simple man like him. He says people are not afraid of a U.S.-led war because they believe Americans will only target Saddam and government sites, not ordinary people. However, he continues in his very broken English, Iraqis are afraid of the aftermath, assuming the country will fragment and dissolve into a vicious civil war.

After I have filed my reports, I join some Canadian colleagues for a late dinner outside the hotel. The restaurant is a dark, smoky place where they serve tumblers filled to the brim with straight gin. Its lack of color is its most desirable quality, since it can pass for water. The conversation takes a distressing turn when it turns out that one of the journalists is delighted he has managed to blackball a colleague. She insulted him somehow in the past and in revenge he showed Iraqi officials transcripts of her reports. She has never been able to get a visa since. Iraqi officials aren't the only ones playing nasty games.

DECEMBER 7, 2002

Iraq hands over to UN weapons inspectors the required declaration on their weapons programs, past and present. It exceeds more than 11,000 pages. The press conference has been delayed several times in the course of the day. Hundreds of journalists champed at the bit inside the Information Ministry until we were finally ordered to get in our cars and drive to another ministry complex. This resulted in another high-speed chase through Baghdad's streets ending at a building braced with armed guards. We are locked into an auditorium and told we cannot leave until the proceedings are over. I panic. I am due on the air for *Morning Edition* in a little more than an hour. I race out, jumping over seats and climbing over colleagues, only to find my exit blocked by humorless security. I sputter something. Qadm is there and lets me through. I suspect he thinks I am going to have a complete meltdown.

I'm told later that after I left the situation got completely out of hand. Camera crews pushed and shoved to get into a room where the thousands of pages of documents have been put on display. They smashed down a glass door, but in the end all they saw was volume upon volume labeled "chemical," "nuclear" or "biological," with nothing allowing them to judge the contents. It's going to take days for these documents to be vetted by inspectors and reach the UN Security Council in New York.

Just when the Iraqis look like they are gaining some ground,

Saddam makes an extraordinary and provocative statement through a spokesman on television. I sit taking notes as Sa'ad translates. It's a letter to the Kuwaiti people. Advertised as an apology for the invasion of '90, it's in fact more defiance. True, Saddam does apologize to the people of Kuwait for the pain Iraq's invasion caused, but he still blames the Kuwaiti government and the United States for forcing Iraq to take such extreme measures. He then goes on to say that the Kuwaitis are being had by their leaders, and he praises those who have recently attacked U.S. soldiers who are now massing in Kuwait. When the broadcast is over, Sa'ad clearly approves of what Saddam has said. When I suggest that this may just make things worse, he looks disturbed.

DECEMBER 10, 2002

Diplomatic debates over the degree of Iraq's compliance with UN resolutions continue. It's a good time to get outside Baghdad and go south, where Iraq's Shiite majority is concentrated. Qadm supports my request and offers to help me with contacts, saying with more than a hint of bitterness, "I am a Shiite and one of the few in the Information Ministry." I am surprised at this admission but I don't wish to appear too enthusiastic about his offer of contacts, since he may have been just feeling me out about my real intentions. The Shiite issue is a loaded one and reporters have been warned or even expelled for writing about Iraq's restive majority. In Jordan I have heard stories from Iraqis about increased vigilance by Saddam's security services in the south. Beyond the thousands of U.S. troops poised for a possible invasion, the Shiites constitute the greatest potential threat to Saddam's grip on power.

With the full understanding that it will be difficult, I would still like to tap into this community and see how their memories of the past affect how they think about the present, and I would like to know more about what kind of Iraq they envision in the future. I've asked to go to Najaf, the burial place of Ali, the son-in-law of the prophet Mohammed whose battle in the 7th century over who had the right to succeed the prophet precipitated the major Islamic schism between Shiites and Sunnis. Suddenly tonight Qadm says all trips outside the city are cancelled.

It's late. Given the nine-hour time difference, my deadline for *All Things Considered* is 1 a.m. my time. I'm sitting at my desk in the hotel room trying to weave the bits and bobs I have accumulated into a coherent whole. It's like so many late nights in so many other hotels on so many other foreign assignments. The desk doubles as a dressing table, so there's a mirror in front of me. It's firmly affixed to the wall lest guests try to steal it. At times I put a towel over the mirror since I can't bear to look at myself as I pound away on the computer. Each day I get grayer. I should follow Lorenzo's advice and get some physical exercise, but I forgot to bring a bathing suit with me and haven't had time to go out and buy one.

In many ways covering Iraq is much like covering the former Soviet Union, where I began my career in the late '70s. Then, as now, we all had to live under the close supervision of the security services, in approved housing with approved translators who, like Sa'ad, reported regularly on who we spoke to, where we went, and what questions we asked. I worried then, as I do now, about putting "sources" in danger. There, however, I could speak the language. I could pass for a Russian and stand in shops over-hearing conversations. There's no way here I can pass for an Iraqi, and unfortunately I don't speak Arabic.

Saddam's Iraq is somewhere between Stalin's reign of terror

and the decaying Brezhnev regime. Cracks are appearing. After his efforts at social engineering, when he murdered or resettled restive ethnic groups, Saddam feels the need to woo them with promises of perks, money, and goods if they behave. And for all the ethnic and tribal splits, there is an Iraqi identity that has emerged over time. Like the Soviets, many Iraqis are well educated and proud of their history, and they have aspirations to regional leadership. And like the Soviets, they fear themselves. Again and again they've indicated that they feel they are an ungovernable mixture of peoples who need a strong leader to remain a strong, united country. I would love to corner the foreign minister Naji Sabri and ask him why he has stayed loyal to the man who executed his brother.

It's been almost twenty-five years since I started out as a correspondent in Moscow. I so remember my first day in the bugged apartment, wondering how the hell I was going to cover the country. I still have those fears every time I get a new assignment. The difference now is that I don't blow up as easily. Then I was intemperate, much more insecure, and unnecessarily aggressive in the way I dealt with Soviet officials, not to mention the people I worked with. I like getting older, even if I don't like looking in the mirror.

Life doesn't turn out at all how you expect it. I never intended to be a correspondent. I started behind the scenes as a production assistant and was propelled in front of the camera because ABC News figured I spoke some Russian and a vice president had the audacity to think I might do something that other correspondents they had sent to Moscow would not. I thought I would have kids. I didn't, and I would not be doing what I am doing now if I had. With rare exceptions, the women who do this are single or childless.

And I certainly did not expect to be covering war after war. When I began all this I was covering the Cold War, where I didn't see the heat of battle. True, the KGB roughed me up on a couple of occasions, but reporting out of Moscow in the early '70s and '80s was more a battle of wits. I tried to show how the Soviet regime was corrupted and rotten; the Soviets officials tried to stop me. Eventually they expelled me for my efforts, and I thought I would never be allowed back again. Poor Vint. When we married I was what he fondly called a "TV tart" who made lots of money from the safety of Washington. When I asked him if he would go back with me to the Soviet Union if the Russians ever let me in, he readily promised. There was little likelihood he would ever have to fulfill the pledge.

But the unthinkable happened. I joined NPR, and the Soviet Union fell apart and I was allowed back, and since then wars seem to have become my metier as conflicts have erupted in places no one had heard of before: Georgia, Abkhazia, Nagorno-Karabakh, Chechnya, Tajikistan, Bosnia, and Kosovo. Inadvertently, I became "good" at covering these kinds of situations. And since 9/11 I've spent months in Afghanistan, Pakistan, and the West Bank. Now it's Iraq.

My secret weapon is Vint. He's gone along with this, and the long absences, and given me the security of home and family. When Amer and I grab a few minutes to talk in the parking lot, away from his Japanese and my minder, he keeps asking me how my husband puts up with my work. I tell him we met as grown-ups. Amer has never been outside Iraq, or outside its confines of tradition and family, which are at once alluring and stifling. He is intrigued by my relationship to Vint, which is like nothing he's ever seen. He confesses he is wrestling with an unhappy marriage, but for the sake of his children, he says, divorce is out of the question.

DECEMBER 11, 2002

UN inspection visits are now up to thirteen per day. It's impossible to know in advance where and how far afield the inspectors will go. Reporters who attached themselves to one convoy ended up driving for what seemed like an interminable six hours until they reached an installation close to the Syrian border. The most interesting are the teams looking for chemical and biological weapons. Amer has figured out who's who by watching the license plates and advises me which teams to follow. "I'm a professional," he states simply.

On my first trip, Sa'ad was quite efficient at arranging interviews with a lot of the people I wanted to see, but this time he is merely recycling the same stories. His greed knows no bounds, and our relations are deteriorating. And we have a new problem. He turned up in my hotel room (he has no problem with the guards outside), ostensibly to discuss the next day's program, and then began complimenting me on how smart and energetic I am. Then he really hit home when he told me how attractive I am "for an older woman." I rejected the come-on and ushered him out of the room. He is not pleased that I rejected his advances and is behaving like a punished puppy. However, he has not gone so far as to try to extort sex in return for his continued services. That has been tried by other minders. Another female reporter had problems with a minder down in Basra. He barged into her room, demanding she go to bed with him or he would have her thrown out of the country. She wisely turned to her driver for help. He told the minder he would turn him in if he persisted. The minder backed off, begging for forgiveness, desperate not to lose this well-paid job. I don't want this situation to escalate to the point where I have to involve other officials and draw unwanted attention to myself. As frustrated as I am with Sa'ad, he's still better than the other minders.

I try to go out on my own with the driver as much as I can under the pretext that I want to buy carpets, see art (of which there
is a great deal), or buy supplies. I stroll the sidewalks in Baghdad's thriving Murad Arusafa district, where showrooms are
filled with luxury cars: Land Cruisers for $40,000, top-of-the-line
Mercedes Benz for a mere $72,000. The wealth enjoyed by a
few can be guessed at behind the walls of the villas and mansions of Saddam's favorites. Armani suits and designer dresses
hang in the windows of shops in the Mansour neighborhood.
Where the money comes from for such luxuries can only be
assumed, but nothing in this society is done without Saddam's
approval.

At the other end of the spectrum is Saddam City, the poor
neighborhood on Baghdad's outskirts, home to two million Shiite Muslims. Though I've repeatedly asked permission to visit
this area I have been refused. We drive through without stopping, but I can see mounds of garbage and children playing in its
midst. At traffic lights, war widows, the elderly, and little children come up to the car begging. Had they grown up a generation earlier, these children would have been part of Iraq's wave
of development, a campaign by the Baath Party to improve education, health care, and infrastructure. Saddam's military ambi-
tions and the subsequent sanctions have ended all that. Whom
to blame for this? Saddam or the United States? Many Iraqis just
aren't sure.

DECEMBER 13, 2002

In a land filled with questions about what fresh hell the future
will bring, there is at least one hideaway in the Iraqi capital offering a surprising escape. At the Ghost Music Store the sounds
of the enemy are stacked ten feet high: compact discs of every-

one from Elton John to Britney Spears, the Backstreet Boys to West Life. Sa'ad Yusef, owner of the shop, says he likes music because it connects him to the rest of the world.

Though he's never set foot in the English-speaking world, forty-year-old Yusef has the language down pretty well just from listening to the music. He's proud of his inventory, which includes pop, disco, rap, techno, and alternative rock. Demand is high from Baghdad's urban youth but he says it's not easy to keep the shelves stocked. It's hard to get new material because of the UN sanctions, but he manages to smuggle it in from Jordan and Syria. The CDs are remarkably cheap—about $1.75 each. (Pity they are not my taste.) Asked how he can sell them for so little, Yusef pulls back a curtain behind the counter to reveal a five-bank digital duplicator. He counterfeits.

He photographs the CD covers and reprints them perfectly. Though he understands that the record companies would object, he says Iraqis need these CDs now to survive. The continuing economic sanctions against Iraq have affected its cultural life in many ways. No one can remember the last time a foreign pop star performed here. The Iraqi film industry has all but disappeared, unable to develop what it shoots. By default, live theater is flourishing. Even Saddam Hussein has written a novel, later turned into a play, called *Zabibah and the King*. It's a thinly veiled story of Iraq's trials and tribulations, and it closed recently after a month-long run. Iraqis prefer comedies, lining up to see a hugely popular play called *The Restless* which mocks their miserable situation. More and more, though, Iraqis seek comfort in the mosques.

Praying in the shadow of the renewed UN weapons inspections, Iraqi worshippers mouth one phrase they feel has the power to blow away the looming cloud of war: *"Inshallah"* (it is God's will). Judging by mosque attendance and the number of women wearing head scarves, there has been a dramatic upsurge in religious observance. Saddam has capitalized on the religious wave. A picture of Saddam praying has recently been added to the hagiographic iconography that wallpapers the country. Though once emphatically secular, Saddam launched the so-called Faith Campaign in the '90s to boost his legitimacy at home and in the rest of the Arab world. Saddam University for Islamic Studies in Baghdad is a product of this campaign, and Professor Muhammed al-Sayed is its president.

Seated in his comfortable office, with my minder Sa'ad in attendance, he says the Faith Campaign has helped Iraqis withstand difficult circumstances. He believes it has also given the once strictly secular Iraqi government greater authority in combating crime and corruption, the natural results of so many years of war. And, perhaps most important, he believes that Saddam has neutralized frictions between Iraq's Sunni and Shiite sects by assuming the leadership of all Muslims here. That's the most he will say about the Sunni-Shiite divide. What he doesn't say is that mosques under tight state control have become another vehicle to proclaim Saddam's policies.

Just in case Islam fails them, some Muslims turn to the Virgin Mary for succor. At the Armenian Orthodox Church of Mary in the old section of Baghdad, Muslim women come to pray to the Virgin. An honored figure in the Koran, she is particularly revered here for her miracles, and Iraqis need one right now.

Twenty-nine-year-old Afrar, a Muslim, says she has great faith in Mary. She doesn't think there is a difference between Muslims and Christians. Seated on her haunches, her hands held palm-up in Muslim tradition, she prays in front of a statue of the Virgin. She finds comfort in this church, calling it a house of God. She has turned to Mary, begging for the baby that has so far not appeared, and pleading for protection from an uncertain future.

If all else fails, there is always alcohol to dull the pain. Iraq publishes no statistics on the subject, but according to Mr. Sabri, owner of the al-Mancal Liquor Store, drinking has followed the rising trend of anxiety in a country staggering from crisis to crisis. He offers a range of mind-numbing potions, from top-of-the-line imported whiskeys and Cognacs to locally distilled gin and whiskey. The gin, made from dates, costs a dollar. Locally produced "deluxe" whiskey is a dollar and a half. Locally produced firewater known as *arak* is a mere 73 cents. He says he hasn't taken any particular precautions yet, despite the threat of war, hoping against hope that there won't be one, but he plans to remove the most expensive items for safekeeping in the event things heat up further. A member of Iraq's small Christian community, Sabri, unlike Muslims, is licensed to sell alcohol. Anyone, regardless of religious persuasion, can buy it. But the way it's consumed has changed in recent years, reflecting the shift in Saddam Hussein's policies. Since he proclaimed the Faith Campaign, drinking in public is now banned. The bars and discos that once proliferated are shut. Iraqis say these rules have cut into their fun. Drinking at home is now the norm, but it's just not the same.

When I get back to the Al-Rashid from a day of string-collecting, there is a wedding in full swing in one of the ballrooms. "A wedding without drink. What's that?" asks an Iraqi guest surveying the seemingly alcohol-free festivities. Faez, who has fed and watered me so well in the restaurant, is in charge of the wedding arrangements. I'm not dressed for a wedding but before I can say no he ushers me up to the elegant bride and groom, who are seated on a dais. Once again actions speak louder than words. Here in a country where my government is threatening war, I am welcomed as an honored guest.

DECEMBER 14, 2002

I've managed to squeeze a few extra days out of Qadm, but he says I should not expect more. It's getting on to three weeks since I've been home and I'm frankly not all that sorry that I have to leave. I've done about as much as I can for now and I might as well conserve my energy, since this is likely to get a lot worse. I go through the usual exit preparations but this time all the flights are booked up and I can't get a plane ticket out. Lorenzo and I decide to hire a car and drive to Jordan. When we get to the border, there's the usual two-hour wait as officials check the car, equipment, and documents. Suddenly, though, it appears we have to have an AIDS test because we've been in the country more than ten days. Why you have to have a test as you leave Iraq seems to defy reason, but officials are demanding $200 for the test, and are actually threatening to give us one. The thought of someone sticking me with a potentially dirty needle is not appealing. As I try to figure out how to get out of this I read the handwritten poster on the wall detailing the elaborate exit instructions for foreigners. The key paragraph is midway through. Women over the age of fifty and men over the age of sixty are not required to have the AIDS test. The clear implication is that women over fifty don't have sex. Whatever; I produce my passport to show them how old I am, and the crestfallen officials, seeing their income diminish, grudgingly let me pass. Poor Lorenzo, however, still a sexually active forty-five, has to pay up. At least he persuades them to forgo the actual test.

BRENDA BULLETIN: DECEMBER 17, 2003

And cheers to you all . . .

Brenda, our Eagle of the East, alit last night in the gentle snows of Norfolk some thirty hours after leaving Baghdad. Her plumage is a bit bedraggled, her pintail feathers awry, but homing instinct and humor are intact. In spite of all, she is still one good-looking bird.

For the past three weeks her home away from home has been the Al-Rashid Hotel, made famous by CNN's play-by-play during the first Iraqi War. It is bugged and overstaffed with clumsy security personnel and Brenda's belongings were combed daily. But then, as an almost solicitous afterthought, her door was carefully double-bolted so that no one else, including herself, could reopen it without a special key. She found it amusing if disconcerting to be greeted warmly by her first name by any number of the Iraqi staff whom she had never met.

"Sucking air" is a venerable if somewhat inelegant term to describe the journalistic talent of filling minutes of air time without the support of discernable facts. Brenda sucked a great deal of air in the last two weeks but, as those of you who heard her know, no one does it better. The feeling of the city had changed in the few weeks she had been away from one of defiant nationalism to one of apathetic depression. The people she saw were now tired and resigned. Through gesture and body language, the people of Baghdad conveyed to her the hope that whatever is coming will be short and accurate.

There were two light moments when she left the gloom of impending war. She drove out of the country toward Amman in the company of an experienced Italian journalist whom she had met and befriended in Afghanistan. This gentleman knew how to travel and had a rather more elaborate kit than Brenda's utilitarian bag. Settling in for the long drive, he dug out two quite exquisitely scented baby pillows and something resembling a silk sleeping bag. And then upon reaching the border, she had yet another reminder that she is something of an odd duck in an odd world. There at the crossing was a large sign in fractured English: "Deer Pasingars, All people must have AIDS test except men over 60 and women over 50."

Well, this old geezer is happy to have his crone home.

V

BRENDA BULLETIN: JANUARY 20, 2003

Well, here we go again.

Brenda cruised into Kuwait City today after a disagreeable twelve-hour flight on Kuwaiti Air. The airline, like virtually the entire country, has turned over the actual running of it to other nationalities. The polyglot crew seemed determined to make the experience as unpleasant as possible. She will be there until Friday, when she flies to Amman and then back to Baghdad.

Life in Kuwait centers around the gigantic shopping malls that litter the landscape. The 800,000 Kuwaitis apparently need something to do while the million and a half guest workers do what needs to be done. Brenda has been tempted by certain high-end Parisian outlets not common to our part of the world, but she claims she was able to resist, perhaps because she knows that whatever she buys will have to be lugged into and out of Iraq. One gets the sense that Brenda wants to travel light. She also had some trouble finding many Kuwaitis who were focusing with any seriousness on what may be about to happen immediately to their north.

In her kit when she left, along with all the usual high-tech paraphernalia, were tucked a dozen virgin pristine pillowcases and a full palette of embroidery silk. Only space restrictions saved the sheets from being carted along as well. Those of you who have on occasion observed this aforementioned pattern of her behavior will take solace that, at least for now, she has confined herself to the linens. God help her if she makes a move toward my bureau.

Hope you all had a good holiday season,
V

JANUARY 27, 2003

After a wintry Christmas at home and a warm week of reporting in Kuwait, it's back to Iraq via Jordan. The flight out of Amman is held up until journalists delayed in Paris finally arrive to fill it up. We don't arrive in Baghdad until 3 a.m. We are all in a bad mood and the officials waiting for us are in no better temper. Ahmed, the fixer, now well in excess of 250 pounds, has developed high blood pressure. Carrying Dan Rather's briefcase last week all but finished him off, though he is extremely proud that they got an interview with Saddam. I refrain from saying that I think the interview was obsequious tripe. As another colleague put it, Rather, with his softball questions, might just as well have been interviewing the prime minister of Belgium, not a tyrant who has imprisoned and killed thousands upon thousands of his own people.

At the Al-Rashid the manager whisks me into his office so that I can pay him, and no one else, for a room with a view, the euphemism for a room where the satellite phone will work. There are Christmas cards pinned up on the wall behind him indicating that he is one of Iraq's Christian minority. He asks me for the latest news and says he is terrified that if there is a war, the Shiites will gain the upper hand and purge the remaining Christians, who have reached an uneasy peace with Saddam's Sunni minority.

JANUARY 28, 2003

At the Information Ministry, Qadm is cool. He hints at alleged indiscretions by Kate Seelye, an NPR reporter who has just been in Iraq, and suggests that NPR is in bad odor. Kate did nothing but report the true of feelings of Kurds up north, but her minder ratted on her for asking "inappropriate" questions. Whatever her perceived sins, Qadm's threats are a good way to try to exact obedience from me. As I get my satellite phone unsealed, Mazzin, who's the ministry's equipment guardian, warns me to be careful about using it at the hotel. He says a couple of reporters have recently been expelled for taking their phones out of the ministry building.

Amer is still working for the Japanese, but we catch up in the hallway. He says he will always do what he can to help. He says that nothing much has changed since I was last in Baghdad. I have to have yet another driver, and yet again he's one of Ahmed's relatives. Majed, in his late fifties, is an uncle. We settle into the car and begin the process of divining who's who and how this is going to work out.

Sa'ad, my minder during past trips, has dumped me and will barely speak to me. I wonder if NPR is a pariah, or if my rejection of his overtures is the issue. Amer says Sa'ad is the problem. He apparently overplayed his hand and was caught raking in too much money without sharing it with his superiors, and he has been ordered to cut back on his clients. Qadm assigns me a new minder called Daniella. It's her first time out and she has a distinctly unfortunate ethnic background. She is half-Iraqi, half-Serb, and she declares that her heroes are Milosevic and Saddam. God help me.

JANUARY 29, 2003

Official reaction to President Bush's State of the Union Address last night is predictably negative. Baghdad again insists that Iraq no longer has any weapons of mass destruction and firmly denies U.S. charges that it has links to Osama bin Laden and his terrorist activities in the United States. Baghdad is trying to capitalize on the growing antiwar movement in the United States and Europe and, with the encouragement of Iraqi officials, foreign peace activists are arriving in Baghdad. Today's approved activity is an antiwar rally. However, I suspect it is not what either Iraqi officials or the Greek delegation from Doctors of the World anticipated.

It was billed at the Iraqi Information Ministry as a human chain against the war, but as it turned out, there were only a few weak links. At the Saddam Pediatric Hospital, Greek doctors unfurled a banner saying NO TO WAR, but only a few patients and medical staff joined in. I stood off to the side with young medical students who ignored the proceedings, telling me, deliberately enigmatically, that they hoped for a better life by the time they graduate in June. The parade never mustered enough strength to leave the hospital compound. Greek doctor Nikitas Kanakis was at a loss to explain why more Iraqis did not participate, saying, "It is a strange situation and actually I'm very sad."

Here in Iraq for the first time, another Greek doctor, Kostas Kostanides, told me he was stunned at how numb the population seems after twenty years of political repression, war, and sanctions. He said every time he tried to have a political discussion, Iraqi doctors dodged the subject. I can't imagine that he thought they would act differently. He and his colleagues were clearly uncomfortable at the staged nature of the demonstration, because they said their goal is not to support Saddam Hussein but to oppose war.

A woman who was ushered in front of the television cameras initially wailed on cue when they were turned on, but failed to utter the anticipated anti-Western, antiwar statements. Holding her dying child in her arms, she broke down screaming, "I don't need cameras! I need medicine for my child!" She begged the foreign doctors and assembled journalists to arrange for her child to be treated overseas. Away from the cameras, Iraqi doctors blamed the Iraqi Ministry of Health, not sanctions, for the short-ages. And Dr. Nikitas Kanakis acknowledged he was shocked by how grand the Iraqi government buildings are, while bureau-crats apparently can't come up with funds to buy basic medi-cines with their oil revenues—legal or illegal. But whatever their feelings about the regime, the doctors remain focused on their opposition to a war. Dr. Kostanides said that it's not for people outside to determine the future of Iraq, but for the people of Iraq to decide for themselves.

Saddam Hussein remains in control and his government re-mains defiant. But the views of many expressed off-microphone are now rife with contradictions. More and more make it clear that they want an end to Saddam's brutal hold, but they're also afraid of war and subsequent civil conflict if he goes. And while many say they would welcome outside intervention, these very same people don't believe President Bush's promises that he has Iraqis' interests at heart.

JANUARY 30, 2003

This trip is going to be press-conference hell. Virtually every night there is a riposte to U.S. charges. Iraq is complying to a de-gree with the UN resolution but is playing games over the required reconnaissance flights. Also, Iraqi scientists are not turning up alone for the required interviews. They are insisting they have a "friend" in attendance in order, they say, to ensure that their comments are not distorted. If I were an Iraqi scientist, I would have someone with me too, given what Saddam might do if someone said the wrong thing. The UN inspectors have yet to arrange for Iraqis and their families to leave the country for in-terviews and insist they have not been given the necessary intel-ligence from Washington to back up U.S. claims that there are ongoing illegal weapons programs. Meanwhile, Iraqis live in a twilight between war and peace.

The degradation of Saddam's Iraq can be seen every day, right smack in the center of the city, at Liberation Square. It's been transformed into a vast flea market, with sellers of second-hand clothing, plumbing fixtures, plastic sandals, and cheap Chinese radios. The traders include teachers, engineers, lawyers—anyone seeking a few extra dinars to augment salaries that now average the equivalent of $10 a month. Twenty-three-year-old Alawi, an economics student, has been working in the market since he was fourteen. Standing in front of a table covered with telephones, he insists business is good. Daniella, my minder, is listening to every word, but when pressed on how many phones he sells, Alawi admits that no one is buying telephones.

Most here dispense with the usual praise of Saddam Hussein, whose beaming portrait looks down on the proceedings, but a merchant, Sa'ad Yassin, draws an approving audience when he asks why the United States is targeting Iraq and not North Korea. He gives his own answer. The United States wants Iraqi oil.

In the afternoon, I visit some Iraqis who will dare to see me without a minder. I jump in a cab, ask to go to a restaurant, and then walk on to the house alone. I bring along a stack of magazines that they can't get here. The assembled group includes filmmakers and artists. They prepare *mazgouf*, a local dish of river fish grilled over an open fire. It's a man's job, like barbecuing back home, and to listen to the cook, it requires skill and precision to suspend the fish on sticks and get the flame from pomegranate wood just right. They recall the days when families would stroll down to the Tigris to a row of restaurants serving this delicacy. Now such forays are too expensive, and most of the restaurants are closed. Conversation steers clear of politics— many here have made an uneasy pact with Saddam in order to survive and produce their art. I suspect some present are members of the Baath Party, but that's not a subject they want to discuss. They reminisce about the not-too-distant past, when, they say, Baghdad was like any European city. "We are a place of culture," they explain. They say the city's love affair with books became so well known that people across the Arab world used to say "Cairo writes, Beirut publishes, and Baghdad reads." Inevitably, however, fears about the future seep in. If U.S. troops succeed in capturing Baghdad, as the Mongols, Ottoman Turks, and British did before them, they say they will find a city too proud to welcome an invading force. But these people are clearly torn. They are desperate for an end to the isolation brought on by Saddam's policies. They want to be part of the world again. They want to be able to exhibit their art in Western capitals. But if Saddam goes, they are afraid fundamentalists will move into the power vacuum, isolating them yet again and quite possibly banning the art they love so much.

I come home by cab, hoping I have not drawn unwanted official attention to these people. It's all so familiar, and memories of Moscow flood back. I would do the same thing then: flag a taxi or take the underground to escape my tail. It didn't always work, and I would always warn my Russian friends that seeing me was risky. Once when I was driving my own car, I got lost and drove around and around looking for an exit from the maze of unidentified streets and identical buildings. I noticed I was being followed and finally pulled to the side of the road. "How," I asked my tail in fractured Russian, "do I get to the Ring Road?" The driver answered in perfect English with another question: "Why didn't you ask me twenty minutes ago?" Without further comment, this KGB agent took the lead and guided me miraculously to my apartment.

FEBRUARY 5, 2003

My editor, Doug Roberts, and I discuss the wisdom of reporting on the nature of Saddam's regime at this particular time, but given how much I have broadcast about the weapons issues and diplomacy, we agree it's important to give some context even at the risk of being expelled.

In recent weeks, Saddam has been appearing almost nightly on Iraqi television with his military commanders. New portraits of him have been placed throughout the country, and new songs have been composed in his honor. While there is private grumbling, there are no open signs of dissent.

Saddam in military uniform wielding a gun; Saddam the father patting the head of a child; Saddam looking dapper in a three-piece suit; Saddam in traditional Arab attire defending the Palestinians. He is all things and his image is everywhere. Daniella swoons over one particular portrait, offering the unprompted comment, "He is very beautiful man."

He can be stern, but he is never depicted as the brutal tyrant who has killed thousands of his own countrymen with chemical weapons, shots to the back of the head, or poison. That is the hidden face of Saddam, hidden in the prisons that have no names, hidden in the eyes of the women who not so long ago begged me to find out what had happened to their loved ones who disappeared into Saddam's gulag and have not been heard from since.

Outside the Ministry of Justice, one of my favorite posters shows Saddam holding the scales of justice. All a taxi driver can do is shrug, but that shrug tells volumes. Any number of taxi drivers have now warned it's dangerous to linger too long outside one of the palaces.

I can't say it enough: the power of Saddam Hussein is much

like that of Josef Stalin, a man he is said to revere. He has promised to make his country great. His intelligence services have infiltrated every crevice of his society. Just as the Soviets elevated the childhood snitch Pavel Morozov to heroic status, Saddam has encouraged children to tattle on their parents should they say something the least bit subversive. Western diplomats here in Baghdad say Iraqi officials never come to meetings alone. They are always in pairs, the better to report on each other.

Ahmed al-Shihabi has been painting Saddam Hussein since 1970, when Saddam was clawing his way to power. Al-Shihabi can't recall how many paintings he's done, and he insists artists do this for free, out of love for "Mr. President," as he is called. Architects have also been enlisted into the glorification campaign.

At the enormous Mother of All Battles mosque built to commemorate the Persian Gulf War, the minarets resemble barrels of Kalashnikovs and Scud missiles. Inside the mosque there are 650 pages of the Koran written, it is said, in "Mr. President's" blood. Official legend has it that Saddam donated twenty-eight liters of his own blood over two years to produce the calligraphy. His thumb print adorns a plinth outside, and story has it that another war memorial, an arch with two fists, was based on casts made from Saddam's own hands.

While his image is everywhere, the Iraqi leader has not made a public appearance in almost two years, evidently afraid of an assassination attempt, and until recently he had not been seen often on television. But now there is the nightly Saddam Show. For two hours on a recent evening Saddam listened to his generals, interrupting them to give advice and encouragement. Smoking his trademark Cuban cigar, Saddam gave the impression of calm determination. As if to counter widespread reports that Iraqi soldiers are badly fed, poorly trained, and ill-equipped, the generals described what crack shots their men are. Saddam, the benevolent father, said morale is key and offered homespun tales of how a determined fighter can win, even against a stronger opponent.

In his twenty-three years in power, Saddam has used his strong personality, ruthlessness, and ability to play one center of power against another to retain absolute control. Artist Ahmed al-Shihabi is still banking on Saddam surviving. He's organizing a new exhibition of Saddam portraits at the Saddam Art Center that should open in a few weeks, just when war is likely to start. He points to one portrait manufactured out of shards of aluminum. Saddam glistens in the sunshine and can be reflected by the lights at night. It's a hit, and al-Shihabi is commissioning more, bigger, versions based on the same idea to place on buildings in the city.

And lest anyone in Iraq or elsewhere doubt the future, the news program always closes nightly with a montage of film clips of Saddam accompanied by one of the many ballads praising him. They have one theme . . . that Iraqis want no one but Saddam Hussein and that the people will stay with him to the end.

FEBRUARY 6, 2003

I hang around the Information Ministry until 10:00, the witching hour when Managing Director Uday al-Tae appears. I sit in the office while two babes from French television desperately try to ingratiate themselves with him. They flirt, call in food, offer everything short of a blow job under the desk. After all is said and done, so to speak, I can only mutter something about how important NPR is in the United States. Later, with Qadm, I burst out laughing, saying I am too old to compete with these beauties. I ask him to understand if I don't try. I have to say he seems relieved and happy to receive my discreetly dispensed money without foreplay.

FEBRUARY 7, 2003

Nowhere is Iraq's demise so clear, and so sad, as at the Symphony. The hall is shabby, the red velvet curtain faded. Seated on plastic chairs, the orchestra tunes up—but it's a tricky task. Most of their best instruments were long ago sold abroad. Replacements are costly. Reeds and new strings aren't always available. These musicians play for love. Their stipends have dwindled to $12 a month, so every member of the orchestra has at least one other job to make ends meet. Seventy-year-old Munther Jumil Haffit, chief violist, points to a doctor, an engineer, a retired taxi driver, and a lawyer.

They try to give one concert each month, but sometimes too many musicians miss practice because of work. Yet Munther says that whenever they play, and often there's not much notice, the audience turns up faithfully, and the house is always full.

Abdul Razzaq al-Shekhli, who helped found the orchestra, has been its conductor since 1974. The story of al-Shekhli and his orchestra reflects Iraq's recent history, its development and subsequent decline. In the '60s he had the money to study at the top music colleges in London. His eyes glisten as he recalls those days. Flush with oil wealth, Iraq was joining the developed world. Baghdad was booming. Buildings were going up on every corner. There were extraordinary improvements in education and health care. And his orchestra flourished. By the early '70s it was a full seventy-piece orchestra with more than twenty foreign members, but it's been downhill since 1980, when Saddam launched the devastating eight-year war with Iran.

An Iranian rocket hit al-Shekhli's house, killing his two small children. His wife has never recovered. She still has nightmares. Nothing, he says, seems to console her. Music has helped him, and he hopes his orchestra has helped others get through the difficult times.

It's been a struggle to keep his beloved orchestra together. With Iraq's invasion of Kuwait, the Gulf War, and the subsequent sanctions, the foreign musicians have left. Many of the Iraqi players, his closest friends, have also fled for political and economic reasons. Al-Shekhli can now muster only forty-five musicians. Without a full compliment, he has to rewrite the music to make it possible to play.

Munther Jumil Haffit says he dreads another war. "You are Americans. You can stop it, stop this invasion. You have your own voice." Was this an allusion to the fact that this distinguished man doesn't have his own voice in a police state? He does not, cannot say. It's impossible to know. But these musicians are not defiant. They are sad. Waiting for he knows not what conductor, al-Shekhli says he dares not even hope, and he does not say what he might hope for. "I'm always waiting for hope. We're all waiting for hope."

The musicians just take it day by day. Their next concert, a performance of new Iraqi compositions, is scheduled for February 27. Juggling diplomatic maneuvering and the time it might take for the United States to amass its troops, al-Shekhli thinks the concert might just take place.

BRENDA BULLETIN: FEBRUARY 7, 2003

A Snowy Norfolk day to you all.

Brenda has been in Baghdad for almost two weeks after being in Kuwait City for about one. Both places are bizarre and other-worldly. Brenda has been able to spin out several wonderful pieces that catch the essence of the absurdity that passes for daily life in Iraq, like the one about the expensive, classy emporium in an up-scale neighborhood that imports crystal and elaborate glass chandeliers from France. Commerce elsewhere might be atrophied, but this shop was filled and business brisk. Fragile goblets to toast the night of the cruise missiles, perhaps. She meets a distinguished-looking gentleman inspecting the stemware. He wears a beautifully tailored green outfit with epaulettes but no insignia. She will later learn that this is the Baath Party uniform. Gesturing toward the uniform, she asks, "Is this military?" With barely disguised hostility, he sneers, "No, it is Armani."

In this lull before leaving (she cannot extend her visa and wants to play by the book so that she can get back in later), now is perhaps a good time to talk of Brenda's food groups when working. Basically there are three: caffeine, nicotine, and adrenaline. When on occasion she consumes something more substantial, she dispatches it with such speed that no one has actually observed her eat. Her childhood, though Brit, was not to the best of my knowledge filled with Oliver Twistian deprivation, but you would never know it.

With luck, Mr. Blix will render his report to the UN on Sunday, and Brenda will head back toward Amman. It seems like a lot of reporters are taking off right about then, having made the judgment that there will be a diplomatic delay to the inevitable. NPR wants her to reapply now. The line of NPR correspondents who were all set to go in after her has suddenly gotten very, very short. Maybe, just maybe she gets home for a bit in a week.

Lest you were worried that Brenda has let her embroidery duties slip amidst everything else, be reassured that such is not the case. Her offbeat habits have not gone unnoticed. Indeed, at a press conference at the Ministry of Information, director's chairs were set out, each one stenciled with the organization's name. There, prominently situated between CBS and NBC, some wag had placed a label upon which was printed "Batty babe from NPR: courtesy of the Pew Memorial Trust."

Cheers,

V

FEBRUARY 8, 2003

Today is a national holiday commemorating the 1963 rise to power of Saddam Hussein's Baath Party, whose original ideological objectives were socialism and pan-Arab union. It has since turned into one-party rule where anyone who disagrees with Saddam is ruthlessly purged. Today's celebration coincides with the arrival of UN weapons inspectors on their latest and perhaps final round of talks to try to win full compliance and full explanations from the Iraqis.

The Information Ministry has allowed us to watch the festivities in Saddam's hometown of Tikrit, a special favor since Tikrit is usually off-limits. Reporters in the past have tried any number of ruses to get there, including declaring they needed to go the bathroom while on the road to Mosul further north. Tikrit was once a backwater, but it's immediately clear that this is no longer an ordinary Iraqi town. The tarmac becomes smooth as you approach. On the outskirts there's a huge arched gateway with a massive mural with Saddam Hussein on horseback galloping toward Jerusalem, missiles and warplanes above him. Images of Saddam are everywhere in Iraq, but the number in Tikrit boggles the mind.

While Baghdad may be the capital of Iraq, Tikrit is the heart of Saddam country. It's the Baath party stronghold, and Saddam has surrounded himself with clansmen from Tikrit in his government. The name "al-Tikriti" automatically suggests power and privilege to an Iraqi, and the people here have a lot to lose if Saddam falls. In addition to his massive palace, there are reportedly mansions belonging to his closest associates, but we are not permitted to travel freely in the city. We have been brought here to witness a celebration in Saddam's honor, but it looks like the bloom is off the rose.

There's a veneer of adoration as the thousands of men and women, soldiers and volunteers, who've been bussed in, march across the enormous parade ground—an imposing space that is out of all proportion with the rest of the town. But not even Saddam's loyalists have been able to fill the stands. The empty bleachers say more than the chanting crowds who have turned up repeating again and again, "We give our blood and soul for Saddam."

Saddam still has hysterical supporters, akin to those who clung to Stalin, but once again I'm reminded of the waning days of the Soviet Union, when crowds came out for the command performances but only because they had to. Even with a war looming, the volunteer army is a pretty lackluster group. There are men in green fatigues carrying old, worn guns. They don't even have boots on, just normal shoes. The women wear long skirts skimming high heels or more comfortable sneakers. Some carry weapons, but while a few insist, "We have regular training and are all crack shots," others confess they've never touched a weapon before and have been dragged in for the parade from school along with classmates.

A teacher, who was in the stands, was delighted to practice her English. Asked if she might contact me at the hotel in Baghdad, I said, "Of course." Minutes later she ran up to me, embarrassed—she gave me back my business card, saying it had been a terrible mistake to think she could see me. Clearly, someone had gotten to her. She didn't dare even hold on to my name and address.

FEBRUARY 10, 2003

It's that time again. I pay up the vast bill for services not rendered at the Information Ministry, seal up the phone, get the exit-permission letters, and deposit bags and bags of Iraqi dinars on the cashier's desk at the hotel. Faez and Mohammed, from room service, come up to the room to say good-bye, wondering if I will ever come back, given that war seems imminent. Amer stops me in the parking lot, asking if I will return. I promise I will.

As I leave I am struck by how frustrated and impatient Iraqis have become with the status quo. People want a normal life. They blame both Saddam and the United States for the mess they find themselves in. Some have started to imagine a time when Saddam is no longer in control. As he takes me to the airport, my driver, Majed, dispenses with any caution and says flat-out that the Iraqi military can't do anything; that it's poorly equipped, badly paid, and utterly demoralized. As soon as the bombing starts he's going to put a sheet on his roof for the pilots to see saying WELCOME USA.

BRENDA BULLETIN: FEBRUARY 13, 2003

Well, well . . . sort of . . .

The Norfolk town meeting the other night ran long, as they usually do. When I finally got home, there she was, my Baghdad Bauble, curled and spooned up next to the old Lab, fast asleep. It had been a long slog home, twelve hours from Baghdad to the border by car—once again escaping the now-$250 AIDS test for women under fifty—eight hours in Amman to find an unexpected seat on the next flight out, thirteen hours to New York, and finally the three-hour drive home. She slept through most of it. Her ability to sleep at any time and in any place, but preferably in something that is moving, she claims as her greatest talent. Last year she made a harrowing journey from northern Afghanistan up over the Hindu Kush and down into the Panshir Valley just above Kabul. The pass was at something like 17,000 feet and the main road up had been destroyed by feuding warlords. Brenda and two fellow journalists rented a Russian jeep and started up the mountain on an unimproved track with no guardrails (naturally), which was so narrow and tight that the vehicle could not make the turn at the end of each of the 100 or so switchbacks. The driver was forced to ascend every other switchback leg in reverse. When they finally got to the top some six hours later, Brenda's ashen and quavering mates were appalled to discover that she had literally slept through the whole thing.

The last hours in Baghdad were taken up paying up and paying out with stacks of dinars, the largest denomination of which is 250. Her bill at the Al-Rashid came to $1,200, part of which she paid with dollars, the other part with 1,600,000 dinars stuffed into two enormous shopping bags. With some coaxing, but with a certain pride, she will show you the ugly bruise on her ribcage inflicted when the chair on which she and the dinars were resting collapsed. It is unclear if NPR has a policy covering wounds inflicted by local currency.

The joy of having her here won't last. Her gear has not been stowed but sits in neat piles on the guest bed. Toward the end of next week she goes back to either Baghdad or Kuwait. I hear her now complaining to NPR about the slowness in providing flak jackets and chemical-warfare gear. This is all taking on a sudden grim reality.

V

BRENDA BULLETIN: MARCH 4, 2003

Once again . . .

For the past two days our girl has been in room 726 of the Grand Hyatt in Amman trying to wring a visa out of the Iraqi bureaucracy. By late today it looks as if she has succeeded and will leave for Baghdad in the next day or two. How long she will be there is anyone's guess, but she is going in with a good deal more cash strapped around her waist than in the past. She talks cryptically of being there long enough to see what will happen happen.

The forty-pound Kevlar vest and her oversized Teutonic helmet will probably end up in the storage room of the Grand Hyatt. The Iraqis may not let any of this in, and to say that this gear, at 40 percent of her body weight, hampers movement is something of an understatement. The chemical-warfare equipment is lighter and will go in with her. But it does beg the question of just whose ass all this stuff is meant to cover.

A number of you have written of late questioning the continued use of the Brenda alias. Some have suggested that although amusing at first, the device has become stale, bordering on shtick. Others have written to say that the use of the name Brenda somehow demeans and belittles what she has done and where she has done it. I, too, was wondering about this. When she was here, we talked about it. The long and short of it is that Annie likes Brenda. It gives her a needed distance, a character to play to, and allows humor to seep into situations which, if reported straight, might well bring tears. So Brenda will be with us as long as she wants and needs her, and no longer.

You might be interested to know that Annie was first called Brenda by someone within NPR when she found herself near Grozny in Chechnya, being bombed by the Russian air force in the early '90s. Later a good friend sent her an enlargement of a panel from a Brenda Starr comic book in which a mushroom cloud rises behind Brenda's anguished face. The balloon reads, "Oh, God, there goes my career!" Somehow the name stuck. I hope you understand.

Cheers,

V

MARCH 5, 2003

Back on the road but I can now claim to be an Intermediate Emergency Medical Technician! God help the poor souls who are my first real patients. I spent numerous nights while home attending classes and "sticking" friends so that I now know how to set up and insert an IV as long as I am not in a moving ambulance, there is nothing to distract me, and the patient's veins are popping so I can't possibly miss them. I'm not all too sure such a patient exists.

After weeks, nay months, on the road I arrived home as an intellectual Neanderthal. I had not seen a real newspaper, editorial, or book review, nor had I read any books except my store of background that had something to do with Iraq. I hadn't seen a movie except for repeats of *The Last of the Mohicans* which is a favorite of Saddam's regime and frequently shown on Iraqi television. I was a royal bore. Thanks to Vint, who clipped items he thought would be of interest, I have, at least, caught up a bit on what the "real world" has to offer. However, most of the time when I was home I was fixated on getting back to Iraq.

Since arriving in Amman, all I have done for four days is call Baghdad about the visa. I can't focus on anything else. Qadm keeps telling me, "Tomorrow, tomorrow, tomorrow." To keep my sanity I have started swimming in the hotel pool. I began with ten laps and today topped 120. The rhythm helps to mitigate the strain, but as soon as I dry off I am obsessed again. I live on room service because I won't venture into the lobby, where I will undoubtedly meet up with all the other journalists who have been waiting, unsuccessfully, for a visa. I'm depressed enough and don't need to hear their sad stories too. I can't tell if Qadm is just playing with me, or if he really intends to fulfill his promise. ABC is also waiting, and apparently "The List" of the newly anointed is to appear at the Iraqi embassy on Saturday.

MARCH 6, 2003

The one group which has not had trouble getting visas are the "human shields," peace activists who have offered to stay in Iraq during a possible conflict, but relations are now fraying. Iraq has ordered five human shields to leave the country after a dispute about where they should be positioned to prevent possible U.S. airstrikes.

There are a couple of hundred peace activists in Iraq. They want to choose where they sit out a possible war but the Iraqi authorities have insisted they move to locations the government has selected. These are not the sites many of the peace activists had in mind, and now dozens have chosen to leave, fearing for their safety, and in some cases their integrity. They are staying in downtown Amman at the run-down Saraya Hotel, which has the air of a college dormitory.

They are a real mixed bag, ranging from complete nutters to thoughtful souls. There is no real organization, a range of political views, and now confusion. Many are loath to speak out because while they are obviously uncomfortable with Saddam's regime they don't want to undercut the antiwar movement.

While many dodge me and my questions—they think the press has disparaged them and their efforts—forty-six-year-old Bruce Fortner is willing to speak about the conflict and conflicting emotions. Back in Santa Fe, he had sent out petitions and joined antiwar protests, but he says that just wasn't enough. So in February this lanky carpenter closed up shop and went to Baghdad to support civilians there. He used money raised in Santa Fe to buy medicines for Iraqi children. He wasn't sure how long he would stay. He wasn't at all sure he wanted to be there during a war, and if he did stay he wanted to work in hospitals or orphanages. But after two weeks of wrangling with the activists, the Iraqi authorities announced that the human shields had to take up positions at oil refineries, water and electricity installations, and government communications sites. Fortner found that the decision to leave Iraq was suddenly made very easy. "For me it was pretty cut-and-dried," he says. He had no intention of protecting infrastructure, though he understands those who argue that these places are essential for daily life.

Sue Darling, somewhere in her mid-fifties, is a former British diplomat. She, too, had wanted to be with Iraqi civilians in communities or schools to personalize the face of war by showing that it will be ordinary people who are under attack, but Iraq's choice of sites had also forced her to leave Baghdad. She is nervous about talking to me. She doesn't want to undermine those who have stayed on. She chooses her words carefully. "For myself"—she emphasizes "for myself"—"I felt the direction the action was taking was not what I had personally come for. For me it was more a direct humanitarian movement of being with the civilian population, and it has gone in a different direction."

Darling made the long trip to Baghdad in a convoy of double-decker buses that traveled overland from London. She'd hoped she would be joined by thousands of protesters instead of just the few hundred who've rotated through Baghdad. The mass migration didn't happen, and she is clearly disappointed. And many of those who've journeyed to Baghdad have grown increasingly uneasy as the Iraqi regime has essentially hijacked the peace movement. It decides where activists stay. It pays for their food and lodging, arranges transportation, and provides "minders" who limit their access to the ordinary people they want to protect. And ordinary Iraqis often express ambivalence about the prospect of a war, and that ambivalence is hard for the peace activists to acknowledge and deal with.

When I ask Darling how she reconciles her views about Saddam's brutal regime and her opposition to the war, she cuts off the interview, pushing back her long, graying hair. She's pretty frazzled. She knows time is running out before the war starts, and she doesn't like her options. She says she is thinking about going back.

In the hotel lobby, fliers are stacked on a table. Produced by an ad hoc steering committee, they warn human shields of the dangers. They advise volunteers of the chances of civic uprising, hostage-taking, or the possibility of being tried for treason back home. And the concluding paragraph notes that after the war starts it may be much harder to get out of Iraq than it was to get in.

When I go to transmit my report to Washington, I discover that a key piece of equipment doesn't work. I can't believe it. It worked just fine when I last used it, in February. I change the batteries and play with the cables. Finally I just shake it. Nothing happens. Frantically, I call Washington. We agree that NPR's correspondent Peter Kenyon will fly in tomorrow from Jerusalem with a replacement. Thank god I found out now and not after I arrived in Baghdad.

MARCH 8, 2003

I've got all the equipment problems sorted out, but when I turn up at the Iraqi embassy it appears I am not on "The Visa List," despite Qadm's promises. I have been peremptorily dismissed, but just as I prepare to head back to the hotel pool to drown my sorrow in more laps, a "fixer" from ABC appears. He has helped me in the past. He takes my passport, disappears into an office for an uncomfortably long time, comes back and asks if I am willing to pay $1,000 for a $38 visa. Money changes hands and he tells me to come to his office later that afternoon. I would have happily paid up last week, but last week money wasn't doing the trick.

With vague assurances of a visa, it's time to purchase supplies. I head off to a supermarket and load up on batteries to keep the equipment running, baby wipes for when the water goes, packaged soup should food be a problem, plus cans of tuna fish, jars of peanut butter, Kit Kat and Mars bars, coffee, Coffee-Mate, and cases of bottled water. It's a bit like *Supermarket Sweep*—that game show where you have five minutes to load up your cart. I definitely win the prize for the most money spent in a short period of time, but nothing looks particularly appealing, and I hope I don't have to rely on the odd assortment that I have selected.

I pick up my passport with the visa firmly stamped inside, pack up, check out, and load up the car, which will take me to Baghdad. I join a convoy with ABC, CBS, and a German crew.

MARCH 9, 2003

We hit the border crossing just after midnight and pile into the waiting room on the Iraqi side, where a life-size portrait of Saddam occupies one wall. Over the past months I have spent many an hour looking at this, guessing at what the artist thought with each brush stroke. I wonder if it will still be here when it comes time for me to leave Baghdad. Forms are filled out, cars and equipment are checked and logged, and more money passes between hands. We speed across the desert and the driver wakes me up as we reach Baghdad just after dawn.

At the Al-Rashid Hotel I once again stride across the mosaic of George Bush the elder, which is now discreetly covered with a carpet. (Chief weapons inspector Hans Blix reportedly protested when forced to tread on the former president.) Who will get to steal it, if and when the time comes? The staff greets me like a long-lost relative. Faez, now working the reception desk, asks me, "Are you really staying?" More money is passed as I negotiate for a "room with a view." I am assigned one on an upper floor overlooking the swimming pool with good access for the satellite phone. I hope the bribes mean they will keep their mouths shut when the security guys come round.

As I unpack, I realize that the case with my sat phone doesn't have a seal. I look at the customs form issued at the border. Though I declared it, the phone isn't listed, just my computer. Maybe this is a blessing. I decide that I will not confess to the Information Ministry that I have a phone. I'll save a lot of money, since they charge $100 a day for the privilege of having a sat phone and maybe, just maybe, I'll be lucky if they decide to confiscate them down the road.

While I have been traveling, Hans Blix, the United Nations chief weapons inspector, told the Security Council that Iraq's destruction of thirty-four of its banned Al Samoud missiles was "a substantial measure of disarmament," and he said Baghdad had begun to provide information on its biological and chemical weapons. Mohammed ElBaradei, the chief nuclear arms inspector, was also cautiously optimistic, saying there was no evidence that Iraq had revived its nuclear weapons program. Both said more time was needed, but representatives of the United States, Britain, and Spain are talking of days, not months, before military action.

They have called for a March 17 deadline for Iraq to disarm completely or face invasion, but they have no support for a resolution from Russia, China, or France. This emotional battle in the United Nations goes beyond Iraq to the future of collective action.

I check in with the Information Ministry to get my ID. Qadm looks at me strangely, as if to say, "What are you doing here?" It's clear he never approved the visa, money notwithstanding, and his look suggests he knows I bought my visa in Amman. Bought or not, it is valid, has all the right stamps, and is good for ten days. If there is going to be a war, I hope it starts by then. The ten-day rule still holds and everyone is worried about getting visa extensions. They line up outside Qadm's office, begging, pleading, and paying.

Lorenzo Cremonesi of *Corriere della Sera* is still here, and his hair is wilder than ever. He hasn't had a visa extension in a month and he is living in the shadows. He also no longer has a valid press card, so he can't enter the building and skulks around the parking lot trying to avoid Qadm and his boss, the dreaded Uday. As Qadm negotiates the plight of some journalists, I hear him bark something unintelligible but clearly unflattering about Lorenzo and warn Lorenzo to make himself even scarcer. Just how he has survived so long without being expelled I don't know—and neither does he.

I drop by the NBC office to see Carol Grisanti. She's been here three months without a break because if getting extensions is difficult, getting a new visa is even more problematic. She's clearly exhausted and the hard part hasn't even started. I leave a care package with bath oil, other unguents, and T-shirts for the approaching hot weather. She's writing a situation report for her bosses back in New York. As far as I can tell the situation is utterly confusing, with nothing but rumors and baseless speculation.

The American networks are threatening to pull out if they're not allowed to move their operations from the Information Ministry, a likely U.S. target, to somewhere safer, but the Iraqis are holding firm. With their tons of equipment and satellite dishes, television companies are totally dependent on the largesse of our keepers. I, on the contrary, can broadcast with my sat phone in the privacy of my hotel room, assuming I am not caught.

The press corps, which has now swelled to more than 500, continues to overwhelm the government's ability to provide individual "minders," and without a minder our movements are restricted, and right now I don't have a minder. Daniella, the Serb-Iraqi, has been fired for failing to pay her sponsors a cut of what I paid her. I track down Amer, who's still loyally working for the Japanese reporters. However, they have no taste for war and are planning to leave soon. Amer thinks that when they leave he will be able to be my minder, though he hates to use that word, with all its connotations. He suggests I keep a low profile so Qadm doesn't assign me someone else. This means I will have trouble working for a few days, but it's worth the wait.

In the meantime I have Majed again as a driver. He dares to suggest I pay him directly and not go through his nephew Ahmed. This is the clearest sign yet that the regime is in its final days. Ahmed, with his ministry contacts, has been skimming $80 of the $100 I have been paying Majed.

Majed briefs me on what's been going on. First impressions are that here at ground zero of possible bombardment there is a surreal semblance of calm. Everyone is still going to work and school. Rush-hour traffic clogs the city streets. Construction workers continue to repair the gargantuan limestone-walled headquarters of the Baath Party, which was struck by American cruise missiles in '91 and again in '98 and will more than likely be a target this time. Construction also continues at the Information Ministry.

I get the distinct impression that people have adopted a blind fatalism, but the truth is there's really not much they can do. You would think there would be a run on stores for food and water, but most can't afford these luxuries. They depend on the rations the government has doled out, and they have now been given rations for five months in advance. As a sign of how desperate people are, many are selling their rations in the markets, not hoarding them, because they need money for other essentials like medicine.

We stop by the ration distribution point in Majed's neighborhood. When I drag out my tape recorder, the young men working there say they will fight the Americans to the end. When we get back in the car Majed says, "I know these guys, and how they think, and they won't fight for a second."

Those who have money have scooped up all the generators on the market. People are also buying plastic garbage cans to hold water supplies. Considering that Iraq is one of the world's largest suppliers, there is a shortage of propane gas for cooking. The government appears to have commandeered stocks. Majed tells me in his neighborhood he's seen soldiers pack trenches with propane canisters, presumably so Iraqi forces can explode them as cheap bombs if and when American troops appear. He tells me Baath Party members have been going door to door warning families that they must stay at home in the event of war or else their houses will be destroyed or confiscated as punishment. The party doesn't want the Americans to arrive in a deserted city. Majed observes dryly that you can bet the Baath Party will move relatives to somewhere safe.

We visit some acquaintances who have enough garden space to dig their own small bomb shelter. The kids think it's a great addition, and they rampage around, playing in the tiny fortress. They are too young to remember the earlier bombing raids. Their parents look on, unwilling to tell the children how bad it might be, and they are scared to talk into a microphone about their true feelings. But this extended family, who have warmly welcomed me, is clearly hoping that life will be better before long, as long as they all survive.

I e-mail Vint to tell him I am safe.

MARCH 10, 2003

After so many weeks here on and off, Mohammed, the head of room service, now knows my habits far too well. Concerned because I don't eat breakfast, which is automatically included in the bill, he drops by mid-morning with coffee and fruit. It's also an opportunity for him to ask me, in the seclusion of my room, what I think is going to happen. I don't really have much to offer. He pulls out a photograph of his wife and four kids. He asks if I can help him and his family go to America. I have to explain, as I have done too often in the past, here and in other countries, that I am not an official and have little influence, and I suggest that his timing might not be the best.

My main task today is to avoid the Information Ministry—the feeding frenzy of rumors and the inevitable question, "Are you staying?" I have no idea what I'm doing. Television producers tell me the American networks and CNN had a deal that they would stay together or leave together, but now that agreement is eroding and each organization is deciding its own fate.

I go down to the hotel coffee bar for a cappuccino, or that's what they dare to call it: a confection of instant Nescafé and frothy powdered milk. As I sit there, making lists of things I need to do, I spy a man I know, but I can't remember where I know him from. We lock eyes. He too is trying to figure out why he knows me. We quickly establish credentials. Bruno was in charge of the European Broadcast Union operation in the Russian town of Khasaviurt on the border of the breakaway region of

Chechnya in 1994. The war stories pour out. I spent Christmas and New Year's of '94–'95 there, arriving late one night, after a long, meandering train trip of more than a thousand miles from Moscow, to where Bruno had set up his broadcast base camp. He fixed me up with a bed in the "women's room." The only hitch was that I had to share it with a producer from AP television. It was a little strange to snuggle up next to someone I didn't know with the intimate question, "Do you like the right side or the left?" Stranger still, she didn't bat an eyelid. We were just too exhausted.

Bruno had set up broadcast operations for European and American organizations in a summer camp for wrestlers that clearly was never intended as housing for dozens of journalists in midwinter. In those days, which were not so very long ago, journalists did not have individual portable satellite phones, and we would line up for time on EBU's cumbersome but nonetheless efficient equipment. We went out during the day, collected information, and then returned to base by nightfall to broadcast. You had time to distill your thoughts. There was no instant broadcasting.

The Chechen conflict was the worst either of us can remember. Indiscriminate Russian bombing was matched on the ground by the unpredictable behavior of drunk, unsupervised, terrified Russian soldiers. Bruno and I reminisced about New Year's Eve, the night the Russian troops moved into Grozny. I got caught there as the tanks poured in. The Chechens trapped them in the city streets. They would hit the first and last tanks in a column so the rest couldn't move, and then pick off the fleeing soldiers. Those I later spoke to said they were newly drafted, untrained, and had no idea where they were or what they were supposed to be doing. I spent most of the night hiding in a basement as the fighting went on outside. At dawn, there was a lull. I poked my head out. Buildings all around me had been reduced to rubble. The streets were littered with burned-out tanks and the charred bodies of soldiers. One lone tank was cornered down the street, wounded but not dead, its gun turret desperately flailing as the soldiers inside tried to escape, but there was no way to maneuver out of the trap. Is the fight for Baghdad going to turn into street-to-street fighting, as Iraqis fear?

Chechnya is a reminder of how quickly events take on a life of their own and determine the future. In the beginning, the Chechen fighters had been ordinary residents—teachers, merchants, and doctors—who didn't think they had a chance. Many were fed up with their brief independence, saying it had brought them nothing, but they also resented Moscow's arrogance and blatant racism. They thought they were making an honorable, valiant, short-lived stand against a much more powerful aggressor and were stunned by the Russians' miscalculations and their own successes. In a matter of hours, the brutal battle in Grozny hardened attitudes on both sides and laid the groundwork for the extremism that gradually developed.

While I was in Chechnya, Vint had arrived in Moscow for what was supposed to be a delirious reunion. Instead, he got deliriously sick. While I hunkered down in Grozny, he sat in my Moscow apartment with a raging fever watching *Jaws* in Russian. He claims to have understood every word. Now he waits back in Norfolk.

I call home. We dodge the issue of whether I'm staying or not. I just say I'm taking it day by day. Iraq has destroyed more banned missiles and dismisses concerns about a U.S.-declared March 17 deadline, suggesting that UN weapons inspector Hans Blix might visit Baghdad. A senior Iraqi official has belittled outstanding questions that inspectors have raised about Iraq's arsenal of chemical and biological weapons, calling them "technical details." But he also said that Iraq was preparing for battle.

Just as I turn out the light, Faez calls from the desk. Like Mohammed, he wants to drop by for a reality check. He comes up and asks about the news of the day. His question, like everyone's, is not if there will be war but when.

MARCH 11, 2003

The hotel hop has started. We've all known for a long time that the Al-Rashid might be an American target, and now, with war likely, news organizations are protectively booking rooms elsewhere. Just where might be safe is not clear. I am lumping for the Al-Hamra north of the Tigris River. A number of colleagues are also moving there, so I will have chums. At first the management tells me it's booked up, but a couple of hours later a room is free as NBC checks out to move somewhere else. What do they know that I don't know? As good a friend as Carol Grisanti is, she has her professional secrets. I keep my room at the Al-Rashid but schlep most of my stuff to the Al-Hamra, which I actually like much better. For the same money I have a suite with a kitchenette, which, given the prospects, seems propitious.

When I go down to the lobby to survey the general layout, the day manager points to a notice from the Information Ministry reminding us we are not permitted to have satellite phones in our rooms. This is a gentle coded version of "There will be a sweep so hide it if you have it." The word spreads that tonight is the night. I call NPR and warn them that if they don't hear from me in time for *All Things Considered*, it means I had to hide the phone.

Where to hide the phone? In my underwear? Behind the cushions in the couch? In the oven? No, it won't fit. Then there is the other issue raised by reports of new American weapons that will fry our electronic gear. Word has it that the only way to protect our satellite phones and computers from that threat is to put them in a microwave oven. After all, a microwave keeps the "waves" in, so, it's been argued, it will also keep them out. The rush on the few microwave ovens available in the market turns into a race. I just don't have the energy.

When one lives in a city whose very skyline may look profoundly different in a matter of days, the question "What do you do exactly when bombs begin to fall?" takes on a very real meaning. As far as we know, there aren't any significant government targets around the Al-Hamra, but it is possible that some of Saddam's family have houses nearby, and by afternoon the staff has criss-crossed all the windows with tape to prevent the glass from shattering inward. In the city center, government workers are taking computers out of key ministry buildings, which are likely to be U.S. targets. Most Iraqis intend to hunker down as well as they can.

There are only thirty-four shelters in this large city and most are in elite neighborhoods. Majed notes bitterly that they are only for members of the Baath Party. He says there's no protection in his area. Many Iraqis echo this, saying they have no choice but to seek solace in prayer. And even if there is a nearby shelter, Iraqis don't trust them. They remember all too well the devastating hit on the Amariya shelter in '91 when a U.S. bunker-busting bomb killed 403, many of whom were women and children. It's now a museum, a favorite stopover for minders and a site for vigils by foreign peace activists.

Majed is desperate for the United States to come in quickly. His house was destroyed in the '91 bombing, but he harbors no resentment and wants the Americans to end Saddam's tyranny. At the Tiger Eye liquor store, run by Christians, a salesman avoids political discussion but hands me a stack of calling cards, saying, "Give these to the American troops and tell them we will be happy to meet their needs."

Though dictatorial Iraq strictly limits access to foreign media, it's a poorly kept secret that a small number of Iraqis have access to satellite TV through black-market dishes. They will witness a possible onslaught with one eye on CNN, the BBC, or Al Jazeera, the other on the real thing—that is, of course, if they have a generator and the signals aren't interrupted by sophisticated American weapons.

One Iraqi who Majed and I discreetly visit demonstrates his illegal satellite system. The dish is hidden on the roof beneath a scrim of fabric. "We watch the news every night for every little update," he says, adding, "I don't know whether to laugh or cry, but at least we know what's going on."

Some Iraqis would like to leave the country, but many are afraid even to apply for a passport. Majed says his friend in the passport agency warned him not to apply now because the authorities will consider him a traitor and exact punishment. His son is a police officer, and he tells me the police have been ordered to stay at headquarters twenty-four hours a day. They can go home only to get a change of clothing.

Diplomats are similarly on alert. Most embassies have closed. Those still operating have drawn down their staffs to a maximum of two. Reflecting his nation's reputation for precision, a Swiss diplomat estimates it will take him exactly seven and a half hours to pack, shut up, and move out. He spends most of his time now conferring with other diplomats about the situation. He offers the last of the Swiss chocolate from his stores. He warns of a humanitarian disaster in the wake of war. He sees no evidence that the United States or humanitarian agencies have stockpiled sufficient food outside the country to prepare for the inevitable disruption. He points out that the United States will be responsible under the Geneva Conventions for protecting the civilian population.

The UN inspectors continue their work, but at tonight's briefing it's clear the results remain mixed. They are still waiting for

Iraq's documentation on the disposal of anthrax and VX poison. Iraq promised to produce a letter ten days ago but so far has sent nothing.

MARCH 12, 2003

Reports from the UN suggest the diplomatic wrangling might go on for a while, delaying war until the beginning of April. I don't know how we are all going to last that long. Sanity and dollars are running low. As it stands now, I am positioned for a war to start on the 19th. After that I have to get a visa extension. I am already knackered from the logistics battle, let alone the real one. But I am in better shape than the poor souls who have been here without a break for the past couple of months. One journalist jokes that he's going to start a protest movement for war just to get the waiting and the visa nightmare over with.

"To stay or not to stay?" is the burning question now. The AP has decided to pull its non-Arab staff out of Baghdad and the office is in an uproar. Several who have spent months here covering the story are contemplating quitting over the decision. Once other news organizations hear of AP's decision, they may well follow suit. It is time to discuss this with NPR. I e-mail Loren that I hope my views will be taken into consideration as NPR decides what to do.

I'm still just taking it a day at a time, but now that Amer will be working with me once the Japanese leave, I am much more disposed toward staying. Much as I like and trust Majed, I feel much more comfortable with Amer, who not only is savvy but also speaks good English. I will need him as a combined guide, translator, driver, and savior. The truth of this journalism business, that we are only as good as the people who work with us, has never been clearer.

Loren e-mails back that he needs ammunition to persuade the powers-that-be that I should stay, if indeed that's my decision. I'm surprised and heartened that he is supporting me and trusting my judgment. Gruff as he is on the surface he is no cowboy, and precisely because I know he cares about me I had feared he might just yank me out. But his instincts are that I follow my instincts. I try to muster my arguments. I have Amer. Amer and I have discussed finding some kind of safe-house if things start getting creepy. I am a woman, and an older one at that, whatever protection that might afford me. I might be able to disappear in a *chador* and wait out a war. I seem to have fallen below the official radar. The authorities are much more focused on others, especially John Burns of *The New York Times*, who after weeks cooling his heels in Amman managed to get back in with a peace-activist visa. He has since "legitimized" himself with the Information Ministry, but they hate him for his excellent reporting. As far as I can figure out, the ministry has not bothered to pull transcripts of my reports. I suspect they don't think radio is very important.

But none of this adds up to a hill of beans.

MARCH 13, 2003

The wind whipped through Baghdad overnight, rustling the date trees and coating everything with a dusting of fine sand. Like talcum powder, it insinuates itself everywhere. The gusts are the harbingers of the short balmy spring. It's comfortable sweater weather now, but Iraqis warn of the long, scorching summer with no respite from the 130-degree oven. If war is to come, Baghdadis believe it will have to come soon. Virtually every night, President Saddam Hussein appears on Iraqi television meeting various commanders and promising victory. But for many Iraqis the days are now measured by foreign news broadcasts that crackle over shortwave radios. And then there are the rumors.

It's finally dawning on many here that this could well end up as a fight for Baghdad. And the latest rumor in the capital is that Saddam Hussein will do whatever it takes to fend off the Americans, no matter what the risk to local civilians. Amer tells me the military has laced canals around the city with gasoline to encircle Baghdad in flames and enshroud the city in smoke in a desperate effort to confuse American smart bombs. There's a deceptive veneer of normality to this city of dun-colored houses, suspended between war and peace. The complacency that Iraqis have about America's ability to pinpoint targets is shot through with terror that nowhere in Baghdad might be safe if there is to be a ground war.

The Iraqis take us to see an unpiloted drone aircraft that the United States and Britain claim can deliver chemical and biological weapons. With a wooden propeller and joints stuck together with masking tape, it looks like a toy. Brigadier General Imad Abdul Latif, the Iraqi project director, says the drone performed so poorly on early test flights that it has been grounded.

I call around to all the embassies to see if I can talk to the few diplomats left. I either get no answer or am flatly turned down. A few of us have a meeting scheduled with a French envoy, but when we arrive the *gendarme* at the front desk says the envoy is not available. No apology, no explanation, simply not available. The gendarme says he will never be available.

It is a Shiite Muslim holiday and there's not much official news. I wander the nearby streets and watch as residents prepare the traditional meal. Once this was a community affair. There would be a neighborhood fire, where everyone would gather to cook together, but that was banned by Saddam. In a grudging gesture to the majority Shiites, Saddam now permits them to celebrate in the privacy of their homes. Women draped in black carry pots of soup back and forth between houses. They smile at me but say not a word.

I can imagine the discussions going on back at NPR and e-mail Vice President Bruce Drake, asking that he not make a peremptory decision without at least consulting me first. I just ask that we go day by day.

Majed reminds me that if I am going to stay, I need the same plastic garbage pails every Iraqi has bought to conserve water. We go out on a shopping expedition for yet more water and soda. Prices have doubled in a week; the value of the dinar is dropping by the day.

We pass the zoo, which, given Saddam's son's predilection for tigers, has caused so much sick hilarity between me and Amer. I hope I don't descend to doing the inevitable zoo story. In Afghanistan, the zoo became an easy focus, especially for British reporters, who competed to own the starving blind lion. While Afghans were suffering, *The Daily Mail* demanded that the British government dispatch vets to treat the remaining pathetic animals. The British Defense Ministry wisely decided it would be unseemly to do so.

Every war has a zoo: Sarajevo, Kabul, and now Baghdad. Animals are a lot less demanding an interview than people and a lot easier to access. They don't require that a minder be in attendance. The London *Times* correspondent has predictably done the story, and she generously suggests that I follow suit. The zoo is under reconstruction, but there are apparently two lions and a tiger that the keepers plan to tranquilize in the event of war. The animals got quite upset during the '91 Gulf War and nearly killed themselves trying to get out of their cages. I pass on the story for now.

Sandbags are stacked up near the gates of the Baghdad Museum, where the doors are firmly shut. Curators say priceless treasures have been spirited away for safekeeping, and archaeologists say they're armed and prepared to defend what's left in the museum—as much from possible looting as from American bombing. At the Information Ministry, workers continue to cart out computers and other valuable equipment, but we must still work there.

Majed is sure no one will fight. He recalls '91, when Iraqi soldiers in the capital literally dropped their weapons and fled. As he drove through the city, he and his son collected three Kalashnikovs that had been tossed into the street. He sold two but still has one, which he's kept to defend himself not from the Americans but from possible anarchy. But there are Iraqis who say they will fight the American invaders, and I think they mean it.

Sermons at Baghdad's mosques have become more strident, exhorting Iraqis to fight the infidel. Even if they are initially defeated there are Iraqis who take comfort in their history, insisting they are the toughest Arab people to subdue. Ultimately, they say, no foreigner has been able to control this territory successfully.

MARCH 14, 2003

Qadm has refused to allow Amer to work with me as a minder. He can only be my driver, so I need to find a benign minder to work with us. I have talked to one guy called Sadiq who speaks excellent English. His journalists have pulled out, and he's anxious for more work. He claims to be a closet dissident who has aspirations to be a writer. For now he is "writing for the drawer," as the Soviets used to say. There's something about him I don't entirely trust. Meanwhile the CBC radio correspondent has been told by his bosses that they want him to leave. He is in tears. I feel pretty crass approaching him but nonetheless I ask if I can have the minder he is leaving behind. Saleh is a nice young man who won't get in the way. Amer agrees he is "good," which in this looking-glass world means he is incompetent—just what I want.

The Information Ministry has called in all the minders for a meeting. Amer regales me with the proceedings. All of them are told to be strong and not to look scared. They are reminded to watch our movements carefully and make sure we are not spies working under the cover of journalism. Like petulant little children, the minders all complain about the drivers, saying the journalists let the minders go and then run off with the drivers so the minders don't know what they are doing.

A reporter from *The Boston Globe* is caught with a Thuria, a small hand-held sat phone, and is expelled. The Iraqis are particularly sensitive about these phones because they are easily portable, unlike mine, which though of better quality has a cumbersome and highly visible antenna. They fear that some of us are "spotters" for the American military.

MARCH 15, 2003

While reporters struggle with the dilemma of staying or leaving, Iraqis are facing their own version. Saleh, my new minder, wants his twenty-five-year-old wife and young daughter to go live with relatives far from Baghdad for the duration of any war. His wife has refused. He hopes that I can help change her mind.

The family's two-story cement house looks out on the vast expanse of the Rashid Air Force Base. It was badly damaged in '91 and is certainly destined to be hit again, but Saleh's wife, Esma, is determined to stay with her husband. She pokes her head out of the kitchen and says firmly, "If we're going to die, we will die together." His mother, Sakhara, is on Saleh's side, but so far she's lost the argument.

Though only fifty-two, Sakhara looks much older. Afflicted with high blood pressure and diabetes, her legs are swollen and she moves to the couch with difficulty. I stupidly tell her we are the same age, looking for some common ground, but then bite my tongue. She looks at me sadly, touches my cheek, and then touches her own mottled skin. She says she can't bear to live through another round of missiles and bombs and if necessary will go, alone, to stay with a daughter outside the capital.

If Saleh has his way, and it doesn't look like he's going to, he and his sixty-four-year-old father, Fadl, would stay in the house alone. The house is all Fadl has left from a once-comfortable middle-class life, and he's determined to protect it. His business, a small factory producing metal furniture frames, couldn't survive the sanctions. His savings are gone. The neighborhood reeks of sewage. There were no pipes in better days, either, but then they were on the up-and-up, making improvements. Now the neighborhood has slid into poverty.

Fadl blames the United States and gestures to the portrait of Saddam Hussein that looks down over the dining table. "Saddam is one of us," he says. "He deserves our devotion." Neither Saleh nor Fadl would listen to my suggestion that Saddam had been unnecessarily brutal. They deny that he murdered his own people. Like the Soviets defending Stalin, they insist Iraq needs a strong leader to direct and unite this fractious country divided between competing tribes—Kurds, Christians, Shiites, and Sunnis. Maybe Saddam seems cruel, Saleh concedes, but he has to be. They describe Saddam as an Arab hero who has successfully protected Iraqi sovereignty from outside threats. "We have oil and great riches," Saleh says, "which foreign countries want."

Fadl demands I tell the American people they must use their voice to stop this war. This appeal to public opinion, which is not permitted here, does not strike Fadl as peculiar or ironic. Staring through his thick glasses, he says he will fight to the last, though he acknowledges he has no weapons, just his faith. Eventually he concedes that America has the technology to win militarily. His bravado cracks further when he speaks of two sons who are in the army, posted somewhere in the north. They have not been heard from in weeks. It becomes apparent as the family talks that they have put by very little in terms of supplies and assume the war could be as short as four or five days.

Saleh and his wife are already thinking beyond the war to the cruel summer when Baghdad boils. Assuming there will be significant damage, they wonder how their baby daughter will survive the searing heat and the bugs with no air conditioning, no fan, and no water. As the family's sole breadwinner, Saleh asks if his English is good enough to earn him a job with a future American administration. If surviving means switching allegiances to another leader, even an American, Saleh will do what he has to.

Tonight I did what I had to: I broadcast naked in the dark. Rumors swirled again about a late-night sweep for satellite phones. My thinking went this way: if I turn off the light in my room it's harder to see the antenna on the windowsill and from the corridor there will be no light shining under my door. If someone knocks, I can pretend they have woken me up, beg for a few minutes to get dressed, and then perhaps have enough time to dismantle the phone and hide it. Not a great plan, but the only one I could come up with.

I laid out a dress that I could slip on in seconds, moved the equipment so it was close to the bed so I could quickly push it under the mattress if I had to, and filed my piece in the buff.

Robert Siegel remained in blissful ignorance, and the whole exercise was totally unnecessary as no one came to the door. But they could have, and they still might in the future.

MARCH 16, 2003

An e-mail from Loren is waiting for me when I wake up: "We have won the debate about you staying at least for today." I reply that I want to continue. I have worked so hard to get here, stay here, and arrange all the logistics. I believe it is important to be a witness to whatever happens and to explain how complicated the emotions are here, and, to the degree that I can, explain how Iraqis perceive the situation. I realize it is quite possible that our sat phones will be blocked when the bombing starts, but that doesn't mean there won't be plenty to say when they are up again. And I can't face the idea of sitting on the Jordanian border with hundreds of frustrated journalists massed there, doing nothing. I realize that's not the best reason for staying, but hey.

Amer is now working with me full-time as a driver. I think Majed was happy to be relieved of the job for now. He needs to get supplies and take care of his family, but his nephew, Ahmed, isn't pleased that I have paid Majed directly and not through him, and he now tries to wangle a cut of what I am paying Amer. I let rip. Despite all his family contacts with the Information Ministry, Ahmed has gone too far. In a matter of days or weeks it's more than likely that his ties to the Information Ministry will be a liability, not an asset. Despite all the money we paid him he never delivered on the visas he promised; I got them on my own. If his family feels bold enough to work independently now, I sure do. After feeble protestations he backs off. He clearly realizes it's time to reposition himself if he wants a future.

Logistics continue to be a drain on energy and time. I need to get Amer and Saleh new ID cards, so they are officially working for me. Amer's no problem; he has photographs, but Saleh left them at home, which is miles and miles from the office. When I propose going straight to an instant-photo place, Saleh protests, saying he has to shave first. No, Saleh, you are not going to shave. You are going to get the photo taken NOW. I don't think Saleh and I are going to be working together long. I have a sneaking feeling he is not ready for the rough-and-tumble of war coverage. Am I?

I ask Amer to draw me a map so I can find him and his house if we are separated and telephone connections are disrupted. Addresses alone aren't much use in Baghdad, since street signs are not common. We are still mulling the issue of a safe-house. His family is leaving Baghdad, so I could hide out with him, but the security people know we work together and they might turn up there. He's trying to rent a house somewhere else, but it doesn't look promising. Baath Party members, in their green uniforms, are now patrolling every neighborhood. Amer says the government has placed more intelligence agents in regular army units to prevent defections.

The Iraqis have submitted more documents to the UN weapons inspectors that they say will provide proof that they have destroyed their stocks of weapons of mass destruction. In a last-ditch attempt to forestall war, Saddam Hussein has even admitted that Iraq did have weapons of mass destruction but he says they are no more. There is even talk of inviting Hans Blix back to Baghdad, but this is all too little too late.

People here have little official information about outside events that make war appear imminent—notably President Bush's announcement that tomorrow will be the last day for diplomatic maneuvering to disarm Saddam. All that the Iraqis hear comes in the form of defiant statements from Saddam and his ministers, who vow in increasingly vitriolic language that American troops will be defeated. But the city is rife with rumors, and everyone is preparing for the conflict ahead, talking about what it might mean for them.

We visit a *mukhtar* in one of Baghdad's poorer areas. Abdel Menan al-Drubi is a community leader, approved by the Baath Party. He knows everyone of his 482 charges, and everything about them. Who's married to whom, how many children, who beats whom, you name it. He arrives from one meeting armed with a Kalashnikov, and is about to race off to another. On cue, his children spout the well-worn refrain, "Bush, Bush, listen well, we all love Saddam Hussein." A fifty-nine-year-old former soldier, al-Drubi is quite an impressive specimen, tall and commanding. He says the party has armed all the trusted men in the neighborhood and he insists they will pin the Americans down should they dare to enter Baghdad. Residents have been discouraged from leaving the city, but he acknowledges that people here are too poor to go elsewhere. As we wind up the interview, one of his kids, to whom I've taken a particular shine, gives me a kiss, and al-Drubi says simply, "Take him with you to America."

In off-the-record meetings, weapons inspectors have told some reporters to get out of Baghdad. They may not have found any weapons of mass destruction, but they nonetheless warn reporters that Iraqis may well defend themselves with chemical or biological agents. I decide it's time to unpack my chemical-weapons suit. It's been twelve years since I tried one on—during the Gulf War—and I'm out of practice.

Issued by Communications and Surveillance Systems Ltd. in London (their Web site is Spymaster.com), the suit has the seal of approval of the Israeli army. There are plastic trousers, a smock and hood, booties and gloves, plus a gasmask. There's also a container of decontamination powder. According to the leaflet, the powder is to be sprinkled over any liquid that might collect on the suit so that no drops touch the skin when it comes time to take the suit off. The label says one size fits all, and it might just. On me it is enormous. Style is definitely not a selling point; Mr. Lee Marks at CSS had sweetly warned, "It's not very pretty," and he's right. It reminds me of one of those rubber garments that late-night television commercials promise will make you lose weight in no time.

As I struggle with the mask, it's quickly evident that I would not survive an NBC (military shorthand for nuclear biological chemical warfare) assault. In fact, according to the leaflet, I am already dead, having failed to hold my breath, keep my eyes shut, and secure the mask within the prescribed nine seconds.

I did not go to one of the media boot camps in the run-up to this crisis, because I was simply too busy and, perhaps incorrectly, assumed I knew most of what they were going to teach. Colleagues have said they actually learned a great deal that might improve their chances of surviving a war in Iraq, and as I survey the gear laid out on the floor in front of me, I wish I knew more about the sinister array of chemical and biological substances Saddam Hussein may or may not have in his arsenal. My research material lists blister agents, which cause the skin to bubble and burst, and nerve agents, which send victims into convulsions. Some smell like cut grass, others like burnt almonds. I am not encouraged by one news report that says you're likely to be "doing the floppy chicken" by the time your nose picks up the distinctive aromas.

By all accounts, the most valuable part of boot camp was the combat first aid, and here I'm relying on the tips I've picked up as an emergency medical technician back home in Norfolk, where I am a novice on the ambulance crew: don't use a tourniquet if you can stop bleeding some other way, because, once starved of blood, the affected limb will have to be amputated afterward; never loosen a tourniquet once the bleeding has stopped, because it will just start gushing again; and removing an object that has impaled a friend's flank is a bad idea; you'll just make it worse. I may not get my chemical suit on in time, but I feel pretty good about using the injector of atropine, an antidote which comes with the kit. This skill has won me a couple of new friends in the press corps, who are stunned to learn of my EMT training and swear they will faint if they have to puncture themselves.

MARCH 17, 2003

I log on to find an all-points message from NPR management announcing "time-sheet training." Just what I need right now. Happily, it is cancelled later in the day. In truth, everyone is treating me with kid gloves, so much so that I'm beginning to feel like someone with a terminal disease.

NPR can be an insatiable beast. First there's *Morning Edition,* then *Talk of the Nation* in the afternoon, and then *All Things Considered,* not to mention the hourly newscasts. Given the nine-hour time difference from Washington, this means working a double shift. I work the Iraqi day, to collect information, but I don't finish up until ATC airs at 1 a.m. my time. I haven't been spared a broadcast since I arrived, but I have been spared calls from local stations wanting to do their own interviews. And when I call in to what is known in radio parlance as "record central," the engineers are solicitous. Informed that it is difficult, sometimes impossible, to get through on the congested satellite system, they never put me on hold or ask me to call back.

Loren has also spared me a lot of what must be going on back at NPR, but I sense he's had to cope with endless meetings about my situation. I can only imagine the reaction when management finds out that NBC and ABC pulled out of Baghdad today, with CBS soon to follow. I gather all the news organizations have been conferring among themselves back in New York and Washington, comparing notes on what to do. *The New York Times* and *The Washington Post* are now getting a major case of nerves and are talking about pulling their people out too. If they leave, I can't imagine NPR agreeing that I would stay.

I am sad to find out that a British friend is leaving, but his reasons are more than good. His newspaper is sending in an additional group, among whom there are people "who are not journalists." He's cryptic, but the gist is that the Iraqis would have good reason for suspecting that his team includes spies, and he justifiably feels that his editor has put his life in danger. The European Broadcast Union and my old friend Bruno from Chechnya are also on their way out. The Iraqis have not let them take their equipment with them, however.

There is now a steady succession of convoys of GMC Suburbans heading for the Jordanian border. The normal fare for the twelve-hour journey to Amman leapt from $200 this morning to $500 by noon. By late afternoon the trip topped $1,000, and it is still climbing. Many news organizations have been ordered out following Secretary of State Colin Powell's warning that all Westerners in Iraq are at risk. The Canadian TV team is also pulling up stakes. I will miss them, as they have been among my closest friends here. As far as I can tell that leaves about 150 journalists, with only a couple dozen of them American.

So far, Saddam's regime has not ordered us out. Officials in fact seem to want us to stay, perhaps to fuel the antiwar movement they are banking on, but, as usual, on their terms, and, as usual, they have their own peculiar way of showing their regard. The Information Ministry has now been taken over by intelligence officials. A whole new set of minders has appeared, with benign people like Saleh being let go. I am so glad I went through all the trouble of getting him accredited yesterday! Amer and I confer about what this change will mean. He has a plan and disappears. Hours later, he returns triumphant. He has gone over Qadm's head, and has somehow persuaded someone at the ministry to include him as a minder—but it won't be free. The deal, and there is always a deal, is that we have to get a relative of this official a job with Turkish television, and this means we will have to pay her salary as well. At $200 a month, I figure it's a bargain.

Just when I think I've got logistics sorted out, there's a new wrinkle. The Al-Hamra says all journalists have to leave. On orders from the Information Ministry, we may live in one of three hotels, none of which is particularly appealing. There's my old haunt—the Al-Rashid, rumored to be a target; the Mansour is too close to the Information Ministry and the TV Broadcast Center, other likely targets. That leaves the Palestine Hotel. I've had a couple of rooms booked there protectively, though I'd hoped this dump would not have to be my home. Maybe it was a decent hotel in the '70s, but it has since gone to seed and desperately needs a cleanup, if not a total overhaul. The lobby is oppressive, the red tablecloths in the restaurant are permanently stained, and the soiled walls in the rooms bear telltale marks of where pictures have been removed and furniture shifted.

Amer and I pack up all my stuff yet again, retrieve damp laundry, and transfer everything to the delightful Palestine. Considering the tips I have laid out for each move, my stocks of bottled water are now worth more than fine champagne. There's gridlock in the Palestine's lobby as TV crews arriving with cartloads of gear collide with groups trying to leave.

I drop everything in my room and race out to try to get some last-minute reporting done. I make one last visit to the communications beacon known as Saddam Tower. There's a sky-deck restaurant whose days appear numbered. A few game souls are dining on the last supper, and the Sudanese elevator operator nervously asks what is to happen. The tower rises a full 600 feet over the city and is a testament to Saddam's remarkable ability to snatch victory from the jaws of defeat. At its base a larger-than-life bronze statue of Saddam stands in triumph over disembodied heads of George Bush the elder and Margaret Thatcher, who lie vanquished at his feet. They defeated Saddam and took his tower down, but Saddam put it back better than ever and added his curious interpretation of history. Rebuilt to twice its original height after it was toppled in the '91 Gulf War, the tower would seem to be a prime target once again.

In the shadow of the tower, Iraqis are mobbing pharmacies for medicine and the wait for gas is now five-plus hours. Shop owners and restaurants have emptied their premises of valuables and are locking up. Leading imams have called for jihad, saying the duty of Muslims is to threaten American interests anywhere they can. This follows an edict from Iraq's top Muslim scholars that anyone who provides help to U.S. or British forces will be condemned to hell. This has made some among the Christian minority worry that they might be numbered among the infidels.

Yet at the Catholic Church of the Virgin Mary, Christians and Muslims continue to pray together. Twenty-five-year-old Saheer, in stylish Western clothing, lights a candle alongside her Muslim friend who is dressed discreetly in a long skirt and shawl. Together they pray to the Virgin for peace. There is no talk of victory, no mention of Saddam Hussein. This Christian and this Muslim say they are the best of friends, and that they will remain so.

BRENDA BULLETIN: MARCH 17, 2003

A most welcome call this afternoon. Brenda is well, on her toes, thinking smart, and moving fast, if only to stay a jump ahead of the rumors that swirl like dust.

She phoned in good spirits but guarded, to say that all the remaining foreign journalists have now been moved to the Palestine Hotel for "safety." She would not or could not say how many there were other than "a lot." She had smartly reserved a room in the Palestine after leaving the Al-Rashid en route to the Al-Hamra early last week. She did so to insure that her room had the right orientation for her satellite phone. She talked quickly, quietly, and without lights on so that her antenna would not be spotted. She did say that the Palestine is located "across the river" and that it appears to be in a "safer" neighborhood. But she's seen better accommodations. Then again, she's also seen worse.

I asked for the phone number in the room. "Well, I can't tell you. There is no number listed here in the room. I'd have to go downstairs and ask, and I can't do that." "Why?" I asked. "Because I'm naked." "Naked? Why naked?" She explained that there was another rumor that the secret police were running a sweep of the hotel, looking for illegal satellite phones, and she figured that if a naked woman just out of the shower answered a knock at the door, she might stand a chance.

She has been reunited with the most important asset she could have: a smart and good driver called Amer, the same one she had on her first trip. In the meantime he had been working for some Japanese reporters, but they have all gone home. With his help, Brenda's room is now stashed with crates of bottled water and long-life milk, a lifetime supply of Kit Kats, and trash cans full of tap water for bathing. So there she is on the 6th floor, well-stocked with her dozen yet-to-be-embroidered pillowcases, waiting for what is to happen to happen.

Just to be clear: Annie has been on the Brenda Bulletin list up to this point and, as I wrote recently, she rather enjoyed seeing herself transmogrified into a comic-book character. But I sense, at least for the moment, that this situation might become something quite different. Given the stuff I am seeing on TV—that the Iraqi decision to move the journalists to a central location could be a prelude to taking them hostage—I have decided to take her off the list and drop the use of Brenda. She doesn't need to hear any more rumors from here. She has enough of her own. I have no idea whether she will be allowed to stay. I have no idea what NPR has counseled, but I will talk to them tomorrow. I do know that as of several days ago, she felt her chances were better in a Baghdad bathtub with her Kit Kats than in a convoy of journalists trying to make their way to the border. After Afghanistan, Annie is allergic to gaggles of journalists in convoys.

Let us hope that Brenda will be able to reappear soon. She reminded me just before hanging up that the soft drink of choice in Baghdad is named "Cheer-Up."

Cheers,

V

MARCH 18, 2003

Overnight, President Bush said the Iraqi crisis had reached the final days of decision. He gave Saddam and his sons forty-eight hours to leave Iraq. If they refuse, Mr. Bush said American and British forces massing at the border will wage war "at a time of our choosing." Iraqi officials quickly dismissed the ultimatum, and Saddam was shown meeting with his sons at undisclosed locations in Baghdad. Saddam warned invading troops to expect a "Holy War." With the clock ticking down to tomorrow's deadline, the UN weapons inspectors have pulled out. The last remaining diplomats are following.

Everyone trades what tidbits they know or have heard. A senior Iraqi official told Anthony Shadid of *The Washington Post* he should stay "because there will be no fight and it will be over in days." But who's to say Saddam won't order the arrest of Westerners and deploy them as human shields at potential American bombing sites, as he did with scores of Western businessmen before the Gulf War in '91? I corner Qadm and ask what he thinks. If I am scared, he says, I should leave. He offers no assurances, but I didn't really think he would or could. Nonetheless, I e-mail Loren that I continue to believe I should stay.

It's beginning to resemble a bad episode of *Survivor* as reporters are pulled out, flee, just plain lose it, or defy their bosses back home in order to stay.

Television crews who left last night have reportedly been detained on or near the border by Iraqi security. It's unclear what's going on. In some cases companies failed to pay their bills with the Information Ministry, in part because it was impossible to do so. The fingerless cashier didn't turn up. But we're also hearing that officials are demanding "a currency-clearance certificate," documentation that heretofore had not been required. This bolsters arguments that at this point leaving is as dangerous as staying. *The New York Times* ordered John Burns and his photographer, Tyler Hicks, to find the most expeditious way out yesterday, but both wish to stay and they managed to persuade their editors to delay their departure for several reasons, including concern about possible hazards on the exit route. I keep giving NPR my "just taking it day by day" line, but in fact it may now be too late to leave.

The Information Ministry cashier appears, so just to be on the safe side I shell out the $1,500 fee for the past ten days. If I had declared my sat phone, it would be twice that. I resent having to pay them for the pleasure of censorship but collect the receipts, which I will need if indeed I decide to bolt.

Foxholes and sandbagged dugouts are sprouting like prairie-dog hills around the city. Policemen in helmets direct the diminishing traffic. Iraq's newscasters have yet to report a word of the speech that President Bush gave to the American public last night. There has been nothing about the American ultimatum and nothing about the forty-eight-hour time frame. But Iraqis, so adept at reading between the lines, must have been tipped off that something was awry when Saddam changed tonight from his dapper suits to a military uniform. The city still doesn't look prepared for a full-scale military siege, but it's impossible to determine what military preparations might be going on in the outskirts, since we can't get there.

We are permitted to attend Baath Party demonstrations in the city. The Party members have all donned their green military-style uniforms, but I get a sense of desperation in this crowd of largely overweight bureaucrats, many of whom probably joined the party for job security and advancement. As with the Communists in the Soviet Union, cynicism, self-protection, and self enrichment are the guiding principles.

Some Arab reporters were taken outside Baghdad to see a group of volunteer fighters from France, Algeria, Morocco, and Libya. These fighters claimed they were prepared to blow themselves up following the "Palestinian method." There are some strange types turning up at the hotel who would appear to be more of the same.

With time running out, Bruce Drake, NPR's vice president of news, agrees I can stay at least for now, writing, "I hope you realize I felt it my responsibility to put you and Loren and Barbara [Rehm] to every possible test in making the decision we ultimately make. In the world of clichés the buck stops with me. There is no hour that I do not think about your safety." NPR has never faced anything like this before. I thank him for trusting my instincts, because instinct is all I am working on.

I'm exhausted from discussing the pros and cons of staying. As far as I am concerned, the decision is made. I finally call Vint and ask him if it's OK with him. We don't go into the details. He just says, "I trust you." It is amazing how on the really big things

you don't talk very much. But I know he knew what I was thinking, and he knew I knew, and on and on after so many years, and
many sort-of-similar situations.

MARCH 19, 2003

The city is strangely quiet. Most people simply shrug, as if to say
"We're doing what we can." Instead of praising Saddam, they say
they are trusting in God. Baath Party members have now taken
up positions in every neighborhood. Amer says there are security
and intelligence personnel along with them in the same nondescript uniforms. No one has shoulder boards or name tags. It's
impossible to know who, or what rank, anyone is. They are not a
military force to defend the city, but a blanket of terror to ensure
that people behave. Knowing the price they could pay for saying
the wrong thing, people say little.

While Amer went off to do errands, I took a taxi to and from
the Information Ministry. This is always a good way to talk to
people in private. On the way, the driver had nothing but unpro-
voked praise for Osama bin Laden, declaring that Americans are
anti-Arab and anti-Muslim. On the way back, another driver said
Iraqis know the United States is targeting the regime, not the
people; he then confessed he was terrified that the Baath Party
would try to pressgang his son into the military. This eighteen-
year-old is now confined to the house for his own safety.

CBS is finally leaving. This brings the number of Americans
left to about sixteen. Given all the problems others have had at
the border, they are desperate to unload their undeclared cash,
of which they have a great deal. I am the happy recipient of a
loan of $5,000, which I will certainly need to hang on here.

Once again, just as I think I have everything as organized as
possible, the Palestine Hotel tells me I have to move out. They

declare that they are shutting down the hotel because of the imminent war. I can't bear the thought of moving again, but my protestations go nowhere and I need to get set up somewhere in time for tonight's broadcast for ATC. Several of us pull up stakes yet again and head back to the Al-Rashid.

The staff is still here, but the Russian hookers who provided me with endless entertainment have disappeared. The Internet center is being closed down. Men begin to unplug the computers and pack them into cardboard boxes. The windows have been covered with rugs. As I stand in my room waiting for I know not what, I catch sight of the swimming pool glistening in the dusk. I quickly get into my suit, but when I reach the gate I find the doors are padlocked. I climb over a fence and dive in and just swim and swim and swim. It's a beautiful evening. As I clamber back over the fence, a hotel guard is waiting for me. He motions for me to follow him. I think, "How ignominious. I will be forever known as the correspondent who was expelled for an illegal dip." As we round a corner, he grabs me. All he wants to do is cop a feel. I burst out laughing, which succeeds where words had failed. He flees. I think of how much I would like a hug from Vint. It's pretty lonely here right now.

BRENDA BULLETIN: MARCH 19, 2003

Dear All,

Annie has made her decision. She has convinced NPR that she is safer in Baghdad than trying to make a break for the border—some twelve hours by car under the best of circumstances, which obviously no longer obtain. To their credit her immediate boss and his superiors have backed the idea that it should be Annie's call. Today, I spoke with Loren Jenkins, the foreign editor. He told me of their decision. I agreed. We spoke of other wars in other places and how it always looks more frightening from the outside than from the inside. He said, "Annie makes good decisions and I'll go with her gut."

A raft of rumors and reports from journalists who tried this route over the last forty-eight hours seems to confirm her judgment. Some were detained, some have been reportedly jailed, some strip-searched, some turned back, some relieved of their excess cash for "currency violations." The requisite exit-paperwork that one used to be able to "buy" at the border is no longer available. Order at the border has gone AWOL. In an effort to strip down, the departing CBS crew lent Annie a huge wad of cash. Annie hadn't seen that kind of TV money in quite a while.

We talked at length this morning after her piece on *Morning Edition* aired. The city is partly deserted, many people have left but many remain, the shops are shuttered and boarded. The mood is still, bizarrely, not of a place about to be hit but of a place that is slowly going nuts. There is little evidence of street fortifications or the other things that an armed and defiant populace might do in preparation to resist. Instead of soldiers there are mainly groups of Baath Party bureaucrats in their unadorned insignia-less green fatigues—paunchy fellows who look very uncomfortable and don't seem to know what to do. The place is odd.

Annie and some of the other foreign journalists were moved today from the Palestine Hotel back to the Al-Rashid where she began. Above all she is very, very tired from lugging her gear and her survival rations from place to place, never unpacking. She said an odd bunch of men began moving into the Palestine shortly before she was moved out. Arabs, but who did not look like Iraqis. And then there were the "human shield" folks who have suddenly found themselves in way over their heads. She doesn't know what will happen to them. The staff at the Palestine had been very good to her, but the place was getting spooky.

Despite its proximity to a presidential palace, she thinks that she will be as safe in the Al-Rashid as anywhere. It is well built and sits in a large, open plot of land. Out her window there is a belt the width of "two soccer fields" that was filled somewhat ominously, as we spoke, by a flock of extremely large, dark birds. Just how many journalists are now mustered at the Al-Rashid is hard to tell.

She speaks well of the other reporters she has met: good journalists in a very tight place trying to live up to a high credo. But more important is the small group within the whole. This is a dozen or so friends from other places at other times. They know each other well and trust each other. They know each other's room numbers. They talk a lot together and are a doughty band that will look out for each other. Her driver has a room across from hers. His family has gone to his village. He will help her if needed.

I don't know how much more time we will have to talk or e-mail. The satellite phones may be blocked, and effectively we will be out of communication if they are. I hope to get through at least once more before the deadline. Her gut instinct tells her she was right to stay.

V

DURING

I sleep fitfully for a few hours but by 4 a.m. my time, President Bush's deadline, I'm sort of awake. It's quiet. Nothing. Then at about 5:30, it starts. First there's the wail of air-raid sirens. Red tracers streak through the sky followed by a series of thuds and whomps somewhere in the city. I do a two-way with Robert Siegel but I really can't tell him very much and I have trouble hiding how sleepy I feel. Its foggy and hard to pinpoint what's being hit. Then it's quiet again except for the sound of birds and calls from the mosques.

As I sit on the sat phone waiting to do an update, the hotel phone rings. It's Jon Lee Anderson from *The New Yorker* on another floor. He tells me an Australian colleague has just been told by his defense ministry to get out of the Al-Rashid now because it's a target. I try to digest this information, the hardest yet about the hotel, get back on the sat phone with Robert Siegel, and say as calmly as possible that I can't talk right now because I need to move again.

I haven't unpacked from the last move, so I just lug my bags down into the lobby, where Amer is waiting for me. He can't believe I'm moving again. I can't believe I'm moving again. I'm so tired I can't really think straight, but we head for the Palestine. After several of us had left the hotel yesterday, various television companies had joined ranks and told the Palestine that they would not move. They succeeded where I had not. Now I try to get my room back. New rules. I need permission from the Information Ministry if the hotel is to re-register me. I burst into tears.

Amer and I go to the ministry, where Qadm will not respond to my pleading for a letter. He clearly has other things, like war, on his mind. There has been no official response yet to the first wave of bombing. The rumor is that Saddam is injured, possibly even dead. A group of haggard-looking journalists waits by the TV set for what we have been told will be an important announcement. Finally, three hours after the attack, Saddam or someone posing as Saddam appears on television. We are not granted a private meeting, so we cannot confirm that it is truly him. Whoever it is looks terrible; his face is puffy and he wears thick-rimmed glasses to read a short speech pledging victory.

Amer's observations as usual prove to be the most interesting and illustrative. The Republican Guard has moved into his neighborhood. They first appeared last night to scope out the area. They subsequently returned and broke into three empty houses, where they have now taken up residence. Iraqis had been warned not to leave their houses unoccupied. Amer's neighbors are terrified that the presence of the Guard will turn their area into a battle zone. Amer has moved his wife and three kids out of the city.

Finally Amer and I get the required letter from Qadm and secure rooms on the 6th floor of the Palestine. He will be staying nearby in the hotel from now on. As I move in, who should move in across from me but Qadm! He asks if I have any spare double-A batteries, clearly so he can listen to shortwave radio to find out what's really going on.

There's a second airstrike at night. It's not nearly as bad as I thought it would be and I'm too tired to be frightened. There is simply too much to do.

BRENDA BULLETIN: MARCH 20, 2003

Update.

Annie called not long ago. So far so good. You may have heard her tell Robert Siegel that she had to get off the phone and leave the hotel. At 6 a.m. Baghdad time, information was received that there might well be something underneath the Al-Rashid Hotel that would be of interest to those in the Pentagon responsible for target acquisition. Annie's sister in London called to say that the British press have identified this as an underground bunker of some kind. Annie and her band have now moved back across the Tigris to the Palestine Hotel. The good news is that she was able to take a hot bath even though the water was, for those New Englanders among you, the color of Grade-B maple syrup: i.e., not the molasses color of Grade C but far from the pastel tint of Grade A. She then took a nap. The bad news is that she is now covered with flea bites.

There is a picture of our girl on the front page of the Life section of *USA Today* accompanying an article on the dwindling number of correspondents in Baghdad. Ironically, the photograph of our intrepid lass was taken last year in Afghanistan atop the Hindu Kush at something over 17,000 feet, where she shared accommodations with several goats and a donkey.

I was asked if I wanted to be interviewed for the article as the reporter was interested in how the spouses of these brave journalists are holding up. I turned down the opportunity. What was I going to say? "Oh, I'm just taking care of the home front and changing the diapers on the labradors."

Thank you all for the staggering outpouring of support and love. It has meant so much to us both. I read as many as I can to her rather than jam up her e-mail, which she barely gets time to read. She will get them all when she returns. I will try to answer all of them, but if I miss something, please resend.

Cheers,

V

MARCH 21, 2003

Late last night I was on the satellite phone, barely clothed, in the dark, when I got a phone call from another reporter warning me that security goons were once again searching for our illegal equipment. We are still supposed to keep our sat phones at the Information Ministry. I have long since stopped working there, and given the bombing, and the fact the Information Ministry is a target, just about everyone has moved their phones to the Palestine.

My sat phone is essentially made up of two parts: the antenna and the phone. The antenna, which has three panels that unfold, must be pointed in the appropriate direction, at the appropriate angle for either the Indian Ocean Region satellite or the Atlantic Ocean East satellite. It doesn't work through most windows, so I have placed it out on the balcony, perched atop various suitcases. The antenna in turn is attached by a long cable to the guts of the phone, which sits on my desk. There are more cables from the phone: to my computer, so I can access e-mail; and to a nifty machine that permits me to file voice tracks and tape that sound pretty good (in fact, Vint thinks they sound too good, as if I were in Washington, not Baghdad).

As I race to unplug the antenna I trip on the wire, dragging the antenna off its precarious perch. It hits the cement floor and one of the panels breaks off. I now know exactly what the expression "my heart sank" means. I gather up the bits, hide them, and wait. There's no fateful knock at the door, but how do I tell NPR I can no longer file? There's certainly no way to get a replacement.

This morning, in the daylight, I drag everything out to survey the damage. It's not as bad as what Mike Shuster did in Kuwait. When his sat phone was blown off the roof, the antenna sailed through the air, crashing eight flights down. I get out some tape from my first-aid kit and try to stick the panel back on. It's wobbly, but when I turn the phone on, it works. Later, I get some duct tape from a French TV crew to firmly attach the panel. As I doctor my crippled phone, someone knocks at the door. I panic and stash it under the bed. It turns out it's Amer. We agree on a special knock for the future.

He's found a secondhand kettle in one of the few shops that are still open. He also came across the proprietor of a liquor store who was removing the last of his stock for safekeeping elsewhere. Amer opened the back of his car and told him to just load up. He got a case of red wine (French no less), two bottles of gin, and a case of beer—"medicine," as he calls it. It might be a long time before stores open again.

At the Information Ministry, we're treated to a remarkable performance by Interior Minister Muhammad Diab al-Almed. He appears in Baath Party uniform, waving a Kalashnikov, finger awfully close to the trigger. His vest is bulging with magazines of bullets; at his waist he boasts a rather large knife. There's no sign that he thinks this is theater as he declares, "I have a son who is eighteen and he is also armed, and we will sacrifice ourselves for President Saddam and his family."

We are not permitted to go around the city on our own, and this has severely limited our ability to assess the effects of the bombing. Amer gives me a report of what he has seen and heard. A friend, who did not respond to the call-up for reserves, got a call from someone who did. The unit, working at the al-Taji base, was nearly wiped out by bombing over night. A fellow reporter notes that a Baghdad pop station has been broadcasting the theme song from *Titanic*.

The Information Ministry suddenly offers us a bus tour. We are not told in advance where we are going. We just dutifully pile into the buses. First we are taken to a power station that has not been hit. The intention is for us to see the international "human shields" who have been posted there. This is not very enlightening, though we can see something of the city on the way. Then we are taken to see civilian casualties at a hospital. There aren't many injured, and most appear to have broken legs. Initially they all say they were hit by American bombs, but their injuries and their stories just don't back this up. Many describe being hurt after going outside their houses, either to watch the bombing or to flee. Their houses weren't damaged. They saw no other houses that were damaged. The general conclusion, not the one the Iraqis wish us to reach, is that they were hit by Iraqi antiaircraft debris. That Iraqis are not generally afraid of the bombing confirms its overall accuracy. They see how precise it is. What they are afraid of is what comes next, and what comes next is complicated and dangerous. A lot of people have left the city, including Qadm's family. He offers this up when I ask how his children are, and then he has second thoughts about his admission, saying, "Don't you dare tell anyone."

I have moved yet again, though this time only from the 6th to the 11th floor. The room looks out over the Tigris and the Republican Palace with access to the Atlantic Ocean East satellite, which does not seem to be as congested as others. Getting through on a high-speed line to file quality tracks is getting more and more difficult. The ordinary satellite phone line distorts my voice, making me sound even more tired than I already am.

The lobby of the Palestine is swarming with the remaining journalists and human shields, the group who's come to Baghdad to show their solidarity with Iraqi civilians. Patrick Dillon, an Irish-American in his early fifties, is dressed entirely in black. His head is shaved, and there is a tattoo of crosshairs of a rifle on the back of his skull. He says he served as a soldier in Vietnam and has been obsessed with war and killing ever since. Outside, a group of Korean feminists have raised a banner protesting sexual abuse. Out my window I look at the An Fanar Hotel, where many activists are staying. They have hung a banner from their windows declaring LIFE IS SACRED. No question about it, but what about all the people Saddam has wantonly killed?

I am of many minds about the need and justification for this war. I have seen how brutal Saddam's regime is, but I am not convinced that he continues to have weapons of mass destruction. The United States has not made a persuasive case, and American diplomatic efforts appear lame. I also worry about the U.S. government's staying power to do what needs to be done when it is all over. Americans have shown that they have a very short attention span. My ambivalence, however, makes it easier for me to cover the situation, to just listen to what people here say.

Tonight the bombing was worse than anything we have seen so far. Starting right at 9 p.m., it came in three waves, leaving parts of Baghdad in flames. A cruise missile literally whooshed by my window. Again and again the Americans went back for the hundreds of acres of Saddam's Republican Palace, the showcase of his regime. Deafening blasts came one after another exploding into fireballs. Then there was a lull, then another wave. There were surprisingly few fire engines and almost no ambulances. As John Burns observes, "Any survivors appear to have been left to their fates." Television crews raced to the windows and the roof to film the fireworks. With no explanation, security men swooped in to confiscate their video cameras.

Despite shifting rooms, I am still having trouble getting through on my sat phone. After dialing for more than an hour I realize I am not going to make my deadline, so I finally go down to Larry Kaplow of Cox Newspapers, whose room faces in a different direction. He climbs on a chair and drags his phone out from behind a ventilator grill. Clever fellow. Unfortunately my phone is larger and won't fit there. After scouring every possibility I have decided to tape it under the lip of the bedside table when I'm not using it. It is a real pain setting it up and knocking it down every time I need to broadcast.

MARCH 22, 2003

The Iraqis have set oil fires around the city as Amer predicted. The black smoke has cast a pall, but I can see that the bridges across the Tigris have not been hit. We still have light, power, and phones. So far, this is not as physically arduous as covering the 2001 campaign against al Qaeda and its Taliban protectors in Afghanistan. Then we slept, six to a room, on the floor of whatever accommodation we could find, had no electricity or water, and traveled huge distances on bad roads. Every war has its bizarre characteristics. If the U.S. bombing continues to be as accurate as it has been, the problem for Iraqis may well be the psychological pressure as much as any physical danger. But we are in early days yet.

The command bus tours, announced on short notice, keep us on a very short leash. Late at night the Information Ministry rouses us for another trip. The bus meanders through the city, giving us a glimpse of some of the damage. We pass the smolder-ing Salam Palace, one of the most fanciful of Saddam's cre-ations. Surrounding the central dome, which has now been hollowed out, are four huge busts of Saddam dressed as Saladin, the Mesopotamian warrior who took on and defeated the Cru-saders.

Suddenly air raid sirens signal another attack. Being out late at night, at bombing hour, right next to Saddam's palaces is about as dumb as it gets. I just hope our minders wish to live as much as I do. I swear off any more midnight tours.

We are taken to four houses that have allegedly been hit by American bombs. Iraqi officials set up generators to illuminate the site. They talk of numerous deaths. But once again the stories don't quite add up. The officials say the bombs landed at one time; residents say they landed at another. The officials say several were killed and wounded. Residents say the houses were unoccupied. At a second location, it's the same confusion. I gratefully happen into conversation with an Iraqi Russian speaker; translators are nowhere to be found. He provides an elaborate picture of a happy family sitting down to dinner when an American bomb lands, killing them all. Others, who claim to be relatives of the victims, say no one was killed but some were injured. Once again the damage to the house itself is not consistent with a missile or an American bomb. I retrieve a piece of a shell and later show it to Amer. He says it is from an Iraqi anti-aircraft gun.

BRENDA BULLETIN: MARCH 22, 2003

Saturday, 6 p.m. Annie's gutsy, gravelly reports of the last twenty-four hours have been memorable—she spun out a continuous stream of superb word pictures—but tonight her expected report did not occur. A British reporter in a different location gave the update. I just don't know what has happened.

The onslaught last night literally blew her back into the elevator as it opened onto the 11th floor of the Palestine Hotel, where she and her dirty dozen of old hands are still camped. She got through to NPR on her satellite phone and started to describe the huge billows of smoke and fire erupting from the edifices of Saddam's regime across the Tigris: the immense new palace complex with its distinctive ziggurat. She was trying to answer Washington's queries as to what specific buildings had been struck—all but impossible given the tumult and her own directionally challenged inadequacies—when all of a sudden directly outside the window of room

1133 cruised a very big cruise missile. Now THAT sort of got her attention. Presumably it hung a left at the corner and headed downtown, because by the time she recovered it had disappeared as fast as it had come.

We were able to talk at some length this morning and she tried to allay fears. She said that she believes she has, in fact, an advantage as a woman; the Iraqi secret police don't deal well with a Western "dumb broad." She told the following story: as she was leaving her room last night a large thug of a man wielding a video camera barged in. Assuming that he was a TV cameraman looking for a vantage point from which to film, she lit into him with all the invective she could muster. He retreated in confusion. Only later did she learn that he was in fact a member of the secret police looking for illegal equipment.

Later in the day Annie was still upbeat when she talked to NPR, who relayed the gist to me. Her main gripe was directed toward *USA Today*, who added a year to her age in yesterday's piece. She remains sensitive to this kind of arbitrary behavior, having been mistaken for a seventy-year-old man in Afghanistan.

Lastly, I know that it had to happen, but nonetheless there was a twinge when one of you asked how I was enjoying my role as a lesser Denis Thatcher. . . .

V

MARCH 23, 2003

Suzanne Goldenberg of *The Guardian* is as frantic as I am about the restrictions put on us. She knows a family she wants to visit so we elude the minders at the Information Ministry by sauntering down the street and hailing a taxi. I deliberately don't tell Amer what I am up to, because going to visit families is against current regulations. I have no fear that he would report on me, but he would try to dissuade me from doing something that might complicate my stay here, and if it were found out that he knew what I was doing, he could get into trouble.

The family is scared, so I don't record their voices and I don't reveal their names. They are only seeing us out of friendship for Suzanne. The first words out of the woman's mouth are, "I don't know how much more of this I can take." She and her family have been huddling in one room on the ground floor of a spacious house that could have been transported from Los Angeles. The only difference is that they live next to an Iraqi military base. In the past few days, four cruise missiles have slammed into the installation. With each blast, the woman says the combination of dust, vibration, and noise makes her lose her bearings. She finds herself weeping uncontrollably in their wake. The windows upstairs are broken. The family has covered the furniture with sheets to protect it from falling plaster and shards of glass. Mattresses have been dragged down to an interior room on the ground floor. She coughs. The smoke from the fires set around the city is giving her problems. She asks a friend, who's come to stay, to get some wet towels so she can put them over her face.

Suddenly there's a loud noise. Instinctively the friend jumps back from the kitchen window across the room. It's just the clang of the front gate. The phone rings constantly as relatives check in to make sure everyone is all right. A nineteen-year-old girl, who's also staying here, looks numb. All she can say is that she wants a future but isn't sure she'll live to see one.

As bad as it is, this family says it's still better than during the '91 Gulf War, when electricity, water, and phone lines were immediately cut. But they say the intact infrastructure may be emboldening Iraqi fighters. The family is surprised by the resistance shown by Iraqi troops in the south; they have an illegal satellite dish and have seen reports that Allied forces have faced fierce fighting around Najaf and Nasiriya. Iraqi television has shown video of five captured Americans, one of them a woman. These soldiers don't look very threatening, and this family is wondering how long this will drag on. It's now Day Four, and they have no idea what to expect. That's adding to the psychological toll.

Asked if the armed militias and Baath Party cadres out on the street will fight, the family just shrugs. They heard Saddam's speech in which he said the Americans were lost in the desert. They get the feeling many Iraqis might now think the United States is weaker than they anticipated.

The family goes out sporadically to stock up on fresh food. A few shops are open. There's even a barber who's raised his shutters. In a surprising semblance of normalcy, a garbage truck rumbles by to pick up the trash. But it's far from normal here. The woman's son is not allowed out of the house. He's twenty-two and prime draft material. The family paid a hefty bribe to keep him out of the military but his mother fears he could now be dragged into one of the militias patrolling Baghdad.

While this family and their friends blame Saddam Hussein for many of their problems and believe that Iraq does need a change, they resent what they see as American arrogance. What gives Americans the right to change things that are not theirs to change? they ask. This is a constant refrain. They express pride in Iraq and its history. They are clearly caught in the middle.

Back at the hotel there is a sudden flurry of activity, and reporters surge down to the river. Hundreds of security men are searching for one or two downed American pilots who reportedly ejected over the city and parachuted into the area of the Tigris. Security forces set fire to brush along the banks. Small boats patrol the river with armed militias and volunteers shooting volley after volley into the water. But there's an unspoken tension. As Baath Party members are determined to kill the pilots, other

Iraqis just stand by watching, some quietly giving a thumbs-up as the militias fail. They make it clear that they want the pilots to survive. (As it turns out, there were no pilots.)

Press conferences are now impromptu affairs held in the lobby of the Information Ministry, the better to flee the building should it be hit, perhaps. Looking around at the reporters who are left in Baghdad I am struck by how few Americans there are. Who would ever have thought it would be pared down to sixteen, including photographers, with NPR, *The New Yorker*, and *The New York Review of Books* among them? The absence of CNN, Fox, and the other large American networks has created an intimacy and a lack of hysteria in the coverage. The perception that television is most important, their money, their sharp elbows, their need for pictures, and their shorthand coverage all tilt the way a story is reported. I have to confess that this is a precious time that will undoubtedly never be repeated. Given what little access I have to outside news (at $8 a minute on the satellite phone, I don't log on for long), I really have no idea what the comparatively large numbers of Spaniards, Greeks, French, British, and Italians are producing. I feel as if I am in a cocoon, documenting the small world that I can see.

BRENDA BULLETIN: MARCH 23, 2003

Annie slept soundly through the lullaby of Baghdad last night. Even through the dodgy satellite phone connection, her voice was strong and her mood determined. Like the rest of us, she is seeking some level, some pattern of normalcy in this madness. The very accuracy of the bombardment of Baghdad is having a curious and perhaps unexpected effect. The people with whom she has spoken are on the one hand surprised and appreciative that the "Campaign of Shock and Awe" does not mean Dresden, but neither has it driven that anticipated wedge between them and the regime. It seems almost as if we are not serious.

Her ability to move on her own about the city is curious and unexpected. We talked around the obvious fact that Amer is not always with her. What degree of complicity exists for her solo forays is unclear, but she was able to visit a family on her own to get a sense of the changed mood of the city. There exists something of a pendulum swing. Emboldened perhaps by the fact that they still have water, electricity, and telephones, those she spoke with now feel that they will survive. And there is the fact that at least some of the Iraqi forces are fighting back. This won't be the four-days-and-out scenario that many expected.

Again and again she has been struck by the lack of animosity toward her personally. Indeed quite the opposite. Ordinary people have gone out of their way to be friendly. She was on a bridge observing the crazed mob firing wildly into the Tigris where bailed-out American pilots were reported. Yet another friendly Iraqi came up to her and told her not to worry; those in the mob, he said, were "nutcases."

Lastly, those of you, who like me—and against our better judgment—find it almost impossible to avoid CNN etc. might have come away with the impression that CNN was kicked out of Baghdad over issues involving high journalistic principle. Well, apparently the expulsion had far less to do with principle than with hubris. After its solo run in '91, CNN thought it owned the story, but this time the Iraqis have invited others to watch the fireworks, including Al Jazeera and many European broadcasters. CNN demanded that it be allowed to move its broadcast operations from the Information Ministry, a likely U.S. target, to the Palestine Hotel. A perfectly reasonable demand on the face of it, but there are others in the game this time, who are willing to play by, or work around, the Information Ministry's rules. CNN overplayed its hand. Its demands were met by a flat no, a word they apparently hadn't expected to hear. A heated exchange ensued and the managing director of the Information Ministry ordered CNN out. At the briefing to announce the expulsion there were not a few knowing nods from the Dirty Dozen and others. The remaining press corps has been warned that anyone caught collaborating with CNN would also be expelled.

Annie remains beneath the radar. For today she's OK.

V

MARCH 24, 2003

When I get down to breakfast, or what passes for such at the Palestine, John Burns, *mirabile dictu*, has beaten me to it. That should have tipped me off that something was up, as John works until the wee hours of the morning and is not usually seen until a far more respectable hour. With his halo of tangled silver curls, John is not hard to miss, and his reporting, with its relentless digs at the tyranny of Saddam, has infuriated our keepers. He's been existing on borrowed time, and when I catch him in the restaurant he's deep in conversation with our super-keeper, Uday al-Tae, undoubtedly trying to negotiate some kind of truce. By the time I collect what edibles I can face, their conversation seems to have flagged, so I dare to join. If John has a tempestuous relationship with Uday I have none whatsoever, which can be both bad and good when it comes to the inevitable visa extensions. Uday, as I have mentioned, has an eye for French girls, and my aging feminine charms, lacking a certain *je ne sais quoi*, have not endeared me to him. Neither, however, have I managed to anger him. I figure I'll seize this moment to just say hello. As we sit talking about nothing in particular, a strange-looking creature with glassy eyes appears at the table. He rants on about his wife being taken away in the night. We try to calm him down and establish what's what. It turns out he's Nate Thayer, a freelance journalist, who had slipped in on a tourist visa along with freelance photographer Molly Bingham. They are not in fact husband and wife, but she has indeed been arrested. Nate directs all his comments to me and John, ignoring Uday who, as superkeeper, is the man he should be talking to.

Two other journalists—Matt McAllester from *Newsday* and his photographer, Moises Saman—are also missing. We've known each other since Afghanistan. Overnight I had heard a commotion outside in the hallway. I looked through the peephole and, seeing nothing but the usual thugs, decided it was just another phone sweep. In fact, security was in the process of arresting these friends, who were staying a few rooms away. This morning their room is ominously empty. Nate, the dubious but so far sole source of information, says they are all to be deported to Syria. When we later approach Uday for clarification he won't answer our questions. Qadm similarly has nothing to offer. We are left to speculate on why they were taken. Perhaps they were arrested for visa violations. Perhaps they were caught with Thurias. Their detention sends a chill through the press corps. This is just what we fear most. We wait for news that they have safely arrived in Damascus. In the meantime a French TV crew, which had been picked up by the Iraqis in Basra, is brought to the hotel unhurt, but they have been put under hotel house arrest and are not permitted to work. Their van, with all their equipment, has been impounded. With little else to do, they sit in the overpriced carpet store within the hotel compound puffing on a water pipe known affectionately here as the "hubbly bubbly." It contains nothing more than scented, rather coarse tobacco. Lorenzo Cremonesi, on the other hand, is madly dashing up and down eighteen flights of stairs. Now that the swimming pool, where he once released pent-up energy and frustration, is a

sickly green, he has taken to ascending the hotel heights and
now estimates he has climbed the equivalent of several Mont
Blancs.

Iraqi officials, who brief us on their perception of the overall
situation, seem more upbeat, given the unexpected battles in the
south. The U.S. invasion has been slowed by stubborn resistance
from Iraqi fighters and by a developing sandstorm. Tariq Aziz,
the deputy prime minister, has held a news conference warning
Americans that they were getting themselves into a quagmire.
Iraqis I manage to speak to seem surprised at the durability of the
regime. It does seem that this might go on longer than either we
or a great many Iraqis had initially anticipated.

MARCH 25, 2003

We've settled into a routine of bombing and briefings. The
Palestine can best be compared to a reform school. Amer en-
courages me to at least behave well in public, and all of us dutifully appear at the daily press conferences. Attendance is not
taken, but our keepers appear to keep notes on who is there and
who is not.

Even at midday Baghdad is almost dark, shrouded with thick
smoke from oil-filled trenches deliberately set on fire by Iraqi
forces to interfere with American remote guidance systems.
Streets in the capital are all but deserted as residents watch and
wait for the ground assault to begin. I am having trouble finding
new material that goes beyond official rantings and more "thud,
thud, thud," but my foreign editor, Loren Jenkins, will not listen
to my weary protestations that I have nothing to offer. He tells
me to just keep reporting "all I see, hear, and smell." In a note
fondly signed "The Ogre," he reassures me that I have no idea

how much every little detail is appreciated. I have no way of telling how this is all being received in the States and feel quite isolated from the rest of the war coverage.

There is no sign of the missing journalists, now up to four, in either Syria or Jordan.

MARCH 26, 2003

The wind has been howling. The combination of a raging sandstorm and smoke from the oil fires has turned day into night. With the city bathed in an eerie pinkish-orange haze, Iraqis say they can't ever recall weather like this. Some call it God's revenge on the Americans.

Iraqi television has been hit, and programming was halted for a while, but the main channel is now back on, with endless paeans of praise to Saddam. The Iraqi government clearly anticipated the hit and had mobile broadcast vans ready as a substitute, though it's unclear if broadcasts reach beyond Baghdad. The attack on Iraq's TV stations will resuscitate the debate over the legality of hitting broadcast installations, which started when the United States targeted Serbian TV in Belgrade.

By early afternoon it's started to drizzle. The dust has turned into a mud paste that sticks to everything. The sat phone, out on the balcony, is now covered in a gluey film, but that doesn't appear to have hampered its operation. Suddenly we're told there's been an American attack on a working-class neighborhood called al Sha'ab. Officials are so eager for us to cover this that we are told we don't have to wait for the buses but can go off on our own. Amer and I head out. We stop for directions and are waved away by a policeman, who warns Amer that there are antiaircraft guns in the area and the Americans are going to come back for them. This certainly doesn't jibe with the official version that says there are no military installations in the neighborhood. The policeman doesn't see me because, like everything, the windows of the car are covered in mud. Incidentally, it's illegal to have tinted glass in Saddam's Iraq.

Commercial strips on both sides of a major thoroughfare have been hit by two simultaneous blasts. There are two craters, much smaller than the holes drilled by other American bombs that have fallen in the past week, but the damage is extensive. After a week the war between the United States and Iraq has finally produced an incident with enough civilian victims to create a shock wave of popular protests.

Thirty-one-year-old Abbas bin Ayan was working in his auto-repair shop, one of several small storefronts, when the blasts literally blew him out the door. That he survived is a miracle. There is nothing left of his shop now but a scorched hole. All the bodies have been removed, making it difficult to establish details. Covered in soot, Abbas bin Ayan provides a list of those he knows are dead; three in nearby garages, a twenty-one-year-old in a water-heater shop, a family in one of the charred apartments upstairs. He points to some shards of metal and a pool of blood. He says it's all that's left of a tea trolley and the man who not long before had been catering to local customers. At least ten cars that had been lined up to be fixed have exploded. Faras Rashid had reportedly been working under one. All that remains is a carbonized hulk. A couple who were driving by were also reportedly caught in the conflagration and burned to death.

Residents say they heard fighter planes overhead and several thuds during the morning but didn't pay attention because they had grown accustomed to the bombing and, they imply, to the accuracy of the bombs. The Iraqi information minister has repeatedly accused the United States of deliberately targeting civilians, but people here don't say that. More than anything they seemed disappointed in their misplaced trust in American technology and precision. Surrounded by Baath Party officials who have taken control of the neighborhood, they insist this is a purely civilian area, though one resident quietly points to a nearby stadium where he says soldiers recently deployed antiaircraft guns. This seems to confirm what the policeman told us.

Ambulance workers struggle with fire, hot tangled metal, and the untimely darkness. The rain has converted the veneer of dust to a cloying yellowish mud that now covers Amer, his favorite suit, me, and my microphone and recorder. Amer suddenly looks like an old man. His black hair, mustache, and eyelashes have turned a ghoulish gray from the dust.

A teenager thrusts a can at me. He says it contains the brains of one of the victims. Another shows off a severed hand. "Is this what you call human rights?" scoffs one young man. "Is this what you call liberation?" demands another. "Why must you kill children?" cry others. Like a Greek chorus, conducted by the party faithful, members of the crowd erupt into chants: "Bush, Bush listen well, we all love Saddam Hussein."

Asked how he would respond if American soldiers entered Baghdad, forty-two-year-old Abdel Razek says it's impossible they will reach the city, but he warns that, if they do, the Iraqis will kill everyone they can. A student from the Technological University, who has a rifle slung over his shoulder, says sadly that this war has changed his mind about Americans.

BRENDA BULLETIN: MARCH 26

Annie reports that for the second day running Baghdad has been blasted with a withering sandstorm that has driven inside virtually everyone who remains in the city. In this ugly pea soup, visibility is zero. The building across the street has disappeared. "God," so an

Iraqi told her, "has come to the aid of our country." Yesterday there was a brief break, enough of one for her to see that with the exception of clusters of raggy militiamen digging desultory trenches, the city has emptied out. A few shops opened and then quickly closed. The brief moment of emboldened jubilation following the capture of the first Americans and the "Defend-the-Homeland" enthusiasm has given way to a grimmer anticipation of what is to come. Last night there were renewed strikes close by.

The reporters sequestered in the Palestine Hotel are in a virtual lockdown status. There is a sense that the Ministry of Information, people with whom Annie normally has contact, now have more ominous superiors. Her ability to get out on her own and revisit the families she knows has been strictly curtailed, either by edict or by her own gut judgment. There was a nasty winnowing of the press corps the night before last when several of her colleagues were taken from their rooms, we know not where.

I get the sense that Annie and the Dirty Dozen have seized on this imposed hiatus to catch up and prepare for what is to come. She tucked up on the floor, eschewing the voracious flea-ridden bed, and got some sleep. She and friends have long exhausted her paltry stock of bad wine, but her supply of Cheer-Up and Kit Kats is holding. Her driver, Amer, even managed to find some fresh bananas. This man is now vitally and crucially important to her. All the smart old hands have or would like to have someone like Amer. Her ability to go under and out, if the need should come, will depend on him. We don't talk openly about this, but the inference of mutual support is clear. "How's Amer?" "Oh, things are good, we're working well together." Stuff like that; we don't dare get more specific. It is all in the inflection.

Amer came into her room the other day bringing something. He spotted a photograph of Annie and me taken in the garden here on an opulent summer morning. He went over to the picture, studied every bit of it, and said, "It looks like you have a nice life there, Annie. What are you doing here?"

That pretty well says it all,

V

MARCH 27, 2003

A group of us get together to brainstorm about what we can do to help track down the missing journalists. Larry Kaplow has taken the lead. So far all our efforts to get information from the Information Ministry have been met with a wall of silence. *Newsday* and the Committee to Protect Journalists back in New York are asking everyone from Ramsey Clark to Yasir Arafat to weigh in. A letter to the Information Minister, signed by the Baghdad press corps, is voted down as too provocative at this point. We decide to privately approach another more sympathetic senior official with whom some reporters have good relations.

Phone service has been cut in several neighborhoods as the United States begins to target telecommunications centers. But as Baghdad shudders under the barrage of bombs, Iraqi officials call us to a press conference where the Iraqi defense minister, General Sultan Hashim Ahmed, warned that even if American forces surround Baghdad the ensuing street fighting could last months. General Hashim warned that the invaders would rue the day they entered the city.

There's a run on the remaining drugstores for anti-diarrheals in anticipation that this could be a long siege and that water supplies could be hit next. Though my ironclad stomach is holding out, many journalists in the Palestine are suffering from food poisoning. Iraqis waiting outside shops say there's no Valium available. Pharmacists say it was snapped up long ago by parents who are giving it to their kids, if not taking it themselves.

The hotel is filthy. Trash mounts in the hallways. I have to keep the balcony door open so that the blasts don't shatter the glass. The room is consequently covered with a layer of oily dust. The hotel staff has all but disappeared, and the restaurant has long since dispensed with menus. Instead, it offers up a buffet of gristly mystery meat and glutinous macaroni that never vary. The water, served in commercial bottles, is in fact drawn from the taps. (Another lesson from Afghanistan is to make sure the seal on the bottle-top is unbroken.) When there's time, Amer gets us take-out of chicken tikka and kebabs from one of the few restaurants that are still open. It's a good thing I'm not a vegetarian. The weather is improving, but this only increases fears that the U.S. bombing raids will become more intense.

MARCH 28, 2003

By now I have lost track of what day of the week it is or even what day of the month. I just know it is Day Nine since the bombing started. The *muezzins* have now taken the place of air-raid sirens, their plaintive cries from the minarets echoing through the night.

Another explosion has rocked a crowded street, killing dozens and wounding even more. This is the second deadly blast in a Baghdad marketplace in less than a week; the U.S. military has attributed the first incident to an errant Iraqi missile or deliberate sabotage. Amer and I once again race out. In the dark, a crowd of men move toward the nearby mosque. They carry aloft coffin after rough-hewn coffin, their voices raised in prayer, not pro-Saddam propaganda. The blast hit at 6 p.m., when the local open-air market in the al-Shula neighborhood of Baghdad was packed with shoppers. It's now a mass of corrugated iron, broken glass, and tangled frames of what were once vegetable stalls. A burst pipe does little to wash away the blood, visible in the glow of a flashlight. In the heart of the marketplace people point to a crater about five feet in diameter and a couple of feet deep. They are convinced an American bomb was responsible. It's impossible to know right away, but the extent of the damage suggests something smaller. Amer Dagestani, a businessman who's come to see if friends have been hurt, asks, "Is this the way America brings democracy?"

Shards of metal struck two teenage boys who were standing outside their house at the edge of the market, killing them instantly. Shrapnel peppered the gate behind them, piercing the metal. A third brother standing in the courtyard was hit in the head and also killed. Their bodies are lined up inside, wrapped in white cloth, illuminated by a kerosene lamp. Their father stands frozen, unbelieving, as a friend prays over the dead children. Two surviving sons clutch each other. Their wrenching sobs allow no relief.

In the next room, women draped in black sit on the floor, keening, calling out to God in their grief. Behind them hangs a portrait of Hussein, the prophet Mohammed's grandson, whose martydom in the 7th century is a symbol of the Shiites' suffering. The United States hopes that these Shiites, repressed by Saddam Hussein, will rise up in anger against him, but here in al-Shula the overwhelming emotion seems to be despair.

Families flood into the al-Noor Hospital. The halls echo with desperate wailing as the people call out names, hoping to find their relatives alive. Amer negotiates our way through the crowds. In a simple ward of rusted metal beds, covered with nothing but ratty blankets, fifty-two-year-old Saman Zaki Khadim winces from the bloody wound in his back. Over the hubbub, Amer calmly translates. Saman had been in the market with his son-in-law and grandson trying to buy a TV antenna. He does not lash out at me when he learns I am an American reporter. He just states the facts as he knows them.

The wards are packed. Many of the injured have had to be moved elsewhere. It's impossible to get an accurate count of the dead and wounded. Though a professional, Dr. Ahmed Sufian confesses he's overwhelmed. "All the floor is covered by blood," he says. "Why, why this blood? Even as a doctor I can't understand such things. This is freedom? I don't know."

Amer is silent on the drive back to the hotel. He too is consumed by confusion and despair. It occurs to me that I have never asked him why, exactly, he is helping me. Perhaps he, like me, is struggling to find some truths.

BRENDA BULLETIN: MARCH 28, 2003

I spoke with our girl this morning. She is as fine as can be expected, given what she has gone through of late. She's off on a story, which is why some of you worried when you heard the *Los Angeles Times* correspondent do much of the Baghdad wrap-up this a.m. The mood at the Palestine Hotel is pretty grim as the reality permeates that the 150 or so journalists sequestered there are not getting out any time soon. Many of these journalists are Arabs representing Middle Eastern papers and television stations. Quite a number of them are Europeans, and there are a surprising number from places you would not expect, Greece and Chile among them. The Chileans, in fact, have done a profile/interview with Annie because "Women in Chile don't do this sort of thing."

The last few days have been particularly grueling. An enormous blast occurred in a market the day before yesterday (and another one happened tonight). When Annie arrived with Amer, the light was failing, the sand and smoke swirling relentlessly. In a scene that must have been macabre and horrible in the extreme, she was accosted by screaming, wailing Iraqis brandishing body parts of those killed. I spoke with her later that night after she had had a long soaking hot bath. I am certain she did not notice its color. She was still pretty shaken. She could not talk for long.

The next morning she returned to the scene, where she elicited more facts. Whether the explosion was caused by an errant U.S. bomb or a failed Iraqi rocket is still unclear, but America's image suffers every time something like this happens.

Annie keeps patching together what few creature comforts remain, but the stock is getting thin. She is running flat-out, with repeated filings to NPR each day. She brought with her a copy of Michel de Montaigne's *Essays*. We naively thought it might help pass the time if we read them together and had long e-mail exchanges on nuance and meaning. Hah! That wasn't such a great idea. Neither of us has finished even a single one.

The journalist community at the Palestine Hotel is very much a guy's world divided between print journalists and TV types. Somewhere suspended in her own space is our Annie—neither print nor television; too old to be a babe, too serious to be dismissed—but not really one of the gang, either. And her brutal schedule of constant updates doesn't allow her to socialize much. It doesn't bother her; she works better that way. Moreover, it amuses her to see how the little fissures in the journalistic hierarchy get established. Her main chum of the moment is Tim Judah, who writes for *The Economist* and *The New York Review of Books*. Her attraction for him, however, has more to do with the fact that she is, marginally, more technologically adept and has been able to help him access e-mail.

Every once in a while, despite her efforts to keep a low profile, she gets noticed. She was talking with a senior official of the Ministry of Information. He asked her who she worked for. When she told him, he smiled broadly and said that when he was in America he listened only to NPR.

V

MARCH 29, 2003

The Information Ministry has, at last, been hit. Amazingly, no one was hurt. Our keepers move their operations to the Palestine, and the various TV companies are finally able to move what's left of their gear to the hotel too. Satellite trucks cram the parking lot and camera positions sprout like wildflowers in the surrounding grounds. And the American bombs seem to have resolved the sat-phone dilemma. As long as they are not the dreaded Thurias, they are now openly tolerated at the hotel. I can now broadcast at night with my clothes on.

Deputy Prime Minister Taha Yassin Ramadan praises the first known suicide bomber in this war, who killed himself and four American soldiers in central Iraq. Ramadan identifies the bomber as a junior officer, a father of several children, who blew up a taxi he was driving at an American checkpoint. Ramadan says from now on this will be routine military practice. When I ask if by posing as civilians, these bombers don't put all Iraqi civilians at risk of retaliation by American troops, the answer is a blunt "Not at all." But the incident has unquestionably unnerved American troops and will lead to tighter security in the field.

For all the bombing, a large part of Baghdad, in particular Saddam City, has not been touched. There are no government buildings of note there, and the United States wisely does not wish to antagonize the Shiites who live there, since American officials are hoping they will rise up against Saddam.

Iraqis officials are holding more of their briefings in Arabic, clearly directing their comments to an Arab world that has disappointed them. They are demanding a pan-Arab battle against what they call the lackeys and stooges, a reference to Saudi Arabia, Kuwait, Jordan, and Qatar, which have facilitated the U.S. assault. Some Iraqis, on the other hand, are privately furious that Arabs "on the street" in other countries are supporting Saddam. "Just imagine what they would feel like living under this monster," says one Iraqi.

Opinion here is not black or white. Even those who don't like Saddam resent American interference. And as the war drags on longer than many anticipated, some are feeling a kind of national pride that America has not been able to walk in unopposed. Even those who would like nothing better than to see Saddam overthrown are nonetheless proud that the Iraqi military has put up a better show than expected.

Two Belgian doctors, who've come here as peace activists, post a notice by the hotel elevators offering to help us deal with too much smoking, too much drinking, and too little sex. The turnout at the appointed hour by this usually jaded group is remarkable. The only problem is the doctors don't turn up.

On that note, Amer and I retire to my room to imbibe "some medicine" after I have filed for the evening programs. He's had a crush on a young, beautiful Greek television reporter, for whom he's helped negotiate visas and the like along the way, but he is disturbed that she is now letting herself be used by Iraqi intelligence. It's by no means clear that she really has anything interesting to tell them, but he gets the sense that she tells them whatever she knows in order to ensure her continued stay here, and access. Amer says he's warned her that life in Iraq isn't simple, that she is getting in way over her head, but he says she dismissed his warnings, asserting, "I'll do what I have to, to be a star back in Greece." Whatever romance might have been brewing is over. He asks me if everyone behaves like this. I tell him no.

MARCH 30, 2003

The bombing has been pretty relentless, though no ground attack on the city itself appears imminent. American forces are less than fifty miles from Baghdad now, but they are reportedly strengthening their supply lines while air and artillery strikes grind down the city's defenses. There is talk that the U.S. military underestimated Iraqi resistance. Security is such that I can no longer go out on my own to see families, even with Amer. It is just too much of a risk, if not for me, then for any family I might visit, so Amer and I agree he will do interviews when I cannot. I describe the community I would like to hear from today—Shiite professionals—and I write out the questions.

After he comes back, I grill him on everything he has seen and heard. He reads out his notes, we go back over the details, and the story that emerges is as follows:

Sitting over a cup of dark, sweet tea, thirty-eight-year-old Zanab (this is not her real name) shakes her head in amazement at the events of the past week. She didn't anticipate that Iraqis would take on the Americans with such fervor. She'd planned to sit out this war, watching from the sidelines, expecting it to be over quickly. But now that Iraqis have shown they are willing to fight, this delicate woman in a long blue robe says she too will fight in the streets of Baghdad if American troops try to enter the capital. Pride has overtaken paralyzing fatalism. Zanab is a Shiite Muslim, one of the majority who has endured relentless repression at the hands of Saddam's Sunni-dominated government, but she says the divide, so apparent up until the war, has disappeared under a new unity forged against the Americans. She calls them aggressors who have come only for oil.

She compares the current situation to that of the '91 Gulf War. Then she understood why the U.S.-led coalition pushed Iraqis out of Kuwait. But this time, she says, "We're innocent.

We did not attack anyone." Asked why Shiites are not rising up against Saddam Hussein, as they dared to after the Gulf War, she admits she was initially surprised. But now she concludes the anger against the United States is greater than against Saddam. She says Iraqis are fighting for their country and their faith. People are also very angry about the other Arab countries, she quickly adds. She spits out the names of countries that have done nothing to support the Iraqis or, worse still, who have sided with the United States. Jordan comes in for the harshest criticism. "Just wait," she warns, "we will get out revenge even if it takes thirty years."

Bombs have rained down around her neighborhood. Though it has not been damaged, her typical two-story cement house has shaken so hard that those pictures still on the wall are askew. Last night's attacks were particularly ferocious. Just 500 meters away, the Baghad headquarters of the infamous Ali Hassan Al Majid, Saddam's cousin, was destroyed. Known as "Chemical Ali" for launching attacks against the Kurds, he remains one of Saddam's top lieutenants.

Like many, Zanab expected that the initial wave of bombing would be much worse. As Baghdadis saw the precision of the bombing, they began to believe that the United States would not touch the infrastructure. But by this morning three telecommunication hubs had been eviscerated. Zanab can no longer call out. She can't reach friends and relatives. She feels isolated and sees this as a portent of worse to come.

She lives with her younger brother, his wife, and their small children. It's a modest life, helping with family chores. She has never married, like many women of her generation. Eligible young men her age were decimated by Saddam's eight-year war with Iran. The absence of the usual rote praise of Saddam Hussein suggests no love for him. Her brother, a university student who also runs the family business, is a member of the Baath

Party. He apparently joined more to advance his career than out of any deep-seated loyalty. But now, she says, he's out on the streets carrying a gun and ready to fight. His attitude toward the United States has hardened with the reality of war, the unexpected camaraderie among Iraqis, and reports of bravery from the south.

Yet for all the talk of fighting, she doesn't know how long the family can cope. She fears a siege of the capital. In just one week, the price of food has soared. Potatoes, a wartime staple, have gone up three times, tomatoes and cucumbers five times.

MARCH 31, 2003

The TV station is hit again, but the Iraqis doggedly get what passes for programming back on the air. Another telecommunications building was ripped apart early this morning, the seventh in three days, so phone service across the city, if not the country, is now thoroughly disrupted. This is what really upsets Iraqis.

The deteriorating situation has affected neither official greed nor the government's determination to control us. A notice goes up announcing that we have to get new accreditation cards. The key here is that to get a new ID we have to pay thousands upon thousands of dollars in outstanding fees. And it looks like not every journalist in Baghdad is to be reaccredited. A long list goes up of those who have been "disinvited" to the party. I have survived yet another cut.

APRIL 1, 2003

Amer calls on the hotel phone asking if he can come up, a clear sign he needs to talk about something sensitive that cannot safely be imparted from the lobby. He gives the now-familiar knock. He has heard that the Information Ministry is going to expel John Burns. He says that a vicious minder, out to curry favor with the wickedest of the wicked, wrote a "bad report" about John, saying he had deliberately slipped away on occasions. Amer says John's driver has tried and failed to correct the record.

I track down *New York Times* photographer Tyler Hicks, who says that although John is all right, things are not good. He summarizes a terrifying late-night visit by intelligence agents (which John later described in the paper).

Men in suits and ties, at least one with a holstered pistol under his jacket, said they had known "for a long time" that John was an agent of the Central Intelligence Agency and that he was from that moment under arrest, and that a failure to "cooperate" would lead to more serious consequences. They then proceeded to steal laptop computers, a satellite telephone, cameras, and a printer, plus $6,000 in cash. They left, ordering John to remain in his room until "more senior" intelligence men arrived.

I knock on John's door. I can hear him inside but he doesn't answer. He doesn't appear at the noon follies with the Information Minister. Mutual friends say he will shortly be leaving the country.

Meanwhile, there is good news from Jordan. The missing journalists have surfaced. After eight days in solitary confinement in Baghdad's Abu Ghreib prison, they have been released unharmed, if not altogether unscathed. They lived in uncertainty the whole time, were questioned about their alleged spying activities, and reportedly heard the screams as others around them were tortured. It's unclear who or what was able to secure their release.

It looks like some of Saddam's relatives may have also crossed the border. Amer tells me he has it on good authority, and when he says this I know by now he means it, that one of Saddam's wives and two daughters have left in a convoy for Syria. Officials take the extraordinary step of denying the rumor, which gives it more credence. Amer then goes off to hang out "with the bad guys," to find out what else he can learn.

It's a glorious spring day, and though American troops are closing in on the capital for the Battle of Baghdad, Saddam's propaganda machine is in full gear downstairs, taping one of the pro-Saddam sing-alongs, which air endlessly on television and which are probably now seen by only a tiny fraction of the population. There is a mad dynamic to the cult. Leading musicians have been ordered to the hotel gardens to take part in the production of a newly composed hymn. An enthusiastic man wearing a Saddam button holds a vast placard pointing out the words so everyone can join in. As I record the proceedings, a distinguished-looking gentleman asks if he can help me. He introduces himself as Feodor Embazi, a lute player, age sixty-five. I ask him to help translate the song. He says, "All our songs are love songs for Saddam," adding, "Saddam is with us day and night even in our dreams." I can't tell if he is making fun of the proceedings.

When he finds out I am American, he proudly says his son lives in Chicago, has a green card, and is looking forward to receiving American citizenship. Isn't it strange, I ask, that your son is in America, and you are standing here defending Saddam? "Not at all," he replies, adding simply, "I love my country." I ask if he thinks his son made the right decision by moving to the United States. "Absolutely," he answers.

This seeming contradiction is one that I have heard again and again across the Arab world. The very same people who line up for visas, ready to be the best Americans, could just as well be in the crowds the next day pelting the American embassy with rocks and resentment.

Despite today's unctuous performance, officials have started to mention Saddam less and less by name of late. At most they talk about "the Iraqi leadership." Even when we lob them a soft-ball question about Saddam, which they would have grabbed at in the past, they sort of skip over the subject. Their rhetoric now emphasizes the fight for Iraq, for Iraqi dignity, and for the destiny of the Arab world. Just what this implies about the fate of Saddam is a question no one is able or willing to answer.

Saddam's vast presidential compound, which stretches al-most two miles along the Tigris, came in for more big hits overnight. It's like a huge outdoor movie, and I watch it all from my window. This maze of palaces, barracks, gardens, and out-buildings covers a bunker that was designed by the Germans in the '80s to withstand a nuclear attack. As anxious as Iraqi officials are to show us civilian casualties, they have not permitted us to survey the damage at the palaces.

BRENDA BULLETIN: APRIL 1, 2003

Judged against the grisly end of last week—billowing smoke, driv-ing sand, sheets of rain, mud, screaming Iraqis brandishing body parts—the last few days seem almost benign. For the most part, the people of the city remain remarkably open and kind to Annie per-sonally, spouting anti-American rhetoric only when a Baath Party member approaches. They are fatalistic, but many with whom she has spoken seem to believe that they are not the target, despite what happened last week. What will happen as the noose tightens absorbs all.

Annie took most of a day off over the weekend, slept through most of it, felt better and sounded stronger the next morning. Her spirits as well as her popularity were greatly enhanced when the ever-resourceful Amer got his hands on yet another case of French Bordeaux to go with her remaining bottle of gin and five fresh lemons. How one effectively mixes those ingredients is open to question, but I hope that both the question and Annie were in short order blissfully moot or, if you prefer, mute.

The Palestine, in her words, is like a reform school. The 150 or so inmates (sixteen Americans among them) are let out only under supervision, punished for bad behavior, and watched closely by a growing number of regime officials and security thugs. With the bombing of the Ministry of Information, many of those officials now work in the hotel, using the journalists in effect as unwilling human shields. A quasi-hostage situation? Perhaps not, but there must be disturbing similarities.

Years ago in Moscow in the '70s and early '80s Annie was in a similar situation when the tiny human rights movement was under attack. Andrei Sakharov, one of its founders and a friend of Annie's, was under house arrest in the closed city of Gorky. Annie was being watched and her movements monitored. She could not get to Gorky but she knew Russians who could. So she asked ABC to send her a dozen Super-8 movie cameras (TV then was still collected on film), which she passed out to Russians who went and made some home movies that she found most useful. Now she is working with Amer in a similar fashion. He goes and collects the sound, asks her questions, and is her eyes and ears. That his neck is very much on the line in so doing speaks volumes about the trust that has developed between them. Her piece on Sunday about the conditions faced by an ordinary family was carefully crafted to conceal how it was assembled.

Friends who have watched her over the years have suggested that sometime, somewhere, Annie should have a reunion of all those extraordinary people who, whatever their job descriptions were initially, became over time enduring friends and adopted family. They are unsung heroes, a diverse, brave, and unique group, connected only by their affection for and belief in her.

We spoke yesterday of Peter Arnett, his dreadful lapse in judgment in going on the Iraqi State TV Channel to blast the coalition campaign and his subsequent firing by NBC. What saddened Annie was not so much what he said, but what had happened to the man in the intervening years since his Baghdad heroics of a decade ago. In the time leading up to his ill-advised performance, she saw him as an increasingly desperate, sad old man, angry at being marginalized and given to self-aggrandizement that vitiated what he had been. A cautionary tale for all us old horses. She was much less charitable—in fact, she hooted with laughter—at the report that the Poobah of Kabul, the Wazir of War Correspondents, Geraldo Rivera, was unceremoniously dis-embedded and dumped at the Kuwaiti border for giving away his unit's position by drawing maps in the sand on Fox TV. Annie had seen Geraldo in action in Afghanistan and the picture wasn't pretty. He reported from hostile places where he wasn't, he claimed to be in firefights that were staged, or less than they were cracked up to be, and he recklessly endangered the lives of other journalists by announcing he was carrying a weapon. If his actions were not so intrinsically dangerous, and his employers so supportive, his role of joker would be funny.

V

APRIL 2, 2003

I bump into John Burns in the hallway. He is, as he puts it, "living a clandestine existence, using darkened hotel stairwells in place of elevators, sleeping and working in other reporters' rooms." It is unclear why he has been given even this amount of freedom, as the intelligence guys must know where he is.

Jusef, one of the last remaining waiters, sidles up to me and asks if he can make a satellite phone call from my room. I tell him to come up later in the afternoon. He arrives on cue. He wants to call his brother in Norway to tell him the family is fine.

By now, with phones and Internet out, there is no other way to contact the rest of the world. He looks around nervously, whispering, "Is the room bugged?" I can't give him any assurance it isn't. There's not much I can do if it is. I am hoping that like the waiters, most lower-level intelligence operatives have disappeared, preferring to be with their families than to defend Saddam.

There's a wire report that the United States has hit a hospital. I go out to check. It's not true. Some windows have been blown out from nearby blasts, and some people in the area have been injured, but further questioning reveals that the hospital itself had long since been evacuated.

Outside the hospital there is a pool of blood. Baath Party activists spread the story that a pregnant woman was killed on the spot along with her unborn child. Rumor quickly turns to myth, repeated with ever-growing gore by people on the street, but when we track down an Egyptian watchman who was at the hospital when the bombing occurred, he insists there was no pregnant woman, and no patients at the hospital. A tour confirms that no one has been staying in the hospital for some time. Doctors had refused to work here when the bombing started, well aware that the hospital sits across the street from Saddam's intelligence headquarters. Amer dares not point to the complex, but tells me to look out to my right at a large compound with a gate. It's been damaged. The Baghdad Trade Fair next door, in front of the hospital, has been leveled.

International human shields have continued to stay in Baghdad, assigned to protect power stations and food stores, not working in the hospitals and orphanages as many had hoped. When they get time off, they hang around the Palestine, checking up on the latest news and begging to make calls on our sat phones.

I've been keeping tabs on one shield, in particular: Mark Ubanks, a forty-one-year-old from Warrenton, Missouri. He's personable, with a wry take on what's going on, and we retire to the gloomy coffee shop to catch up. Mark insists he had never taken a political stand before. He says he's never even voted, though he has a curious résumé. He spent four years in the U.S. Air Force, something I don't think he's advertising to his Iraqi hosts. When he left the Air Force, he stayed on in Europe and says he was working as a Web designer when he ended up in Baghdad, as he puts it, "by mistake."

He'd read an article in a Greek newspaper that claimed there were 2,000 human shields waiting in Jordan, with more than a thousand already in Iraq, many, so it said, suffering from diarrhea. Egged on by his Greek girlfriend, he collected medicines. When he arrived in Baghdad, he found there were in fact only a handful of human shields, perhaps no more than 250 at any one time, from as far away as Australia and South Africa. Once in Iraq, Ubanks's opposition to the war prompted him to stay, and the Iraqi Peace and Friendship Society was happy to assign him to protect the Dora power plant. He has to be in place by 8 p.m. every night, in time for the heaviest bombing. While it was initially scary, he says you get used to the bombing, and now after almost two weeks he sleeps through the blasts.

There's a Web site providing instructions on how a potential human shield can get a visa and how to make the trip to Baghdad, but human shields are not an organized group and they are looked on as a bunch of crazies by most Iraqis. Ubanks is frustrated because, with no common voice or leadership, they have been largely ineffective. There are animosities between longtime radicals and newly politicized shields, who, like Ubanks, simply oppose this war. There are shields who are pro-regime and others who are struggling to reconcile their opposition to the war with their distaste for Saddam. These arguments, and the fear of eventual street-to-street fighting, have whittled the numbers down to about forty. The war has gone on a lot longer than

Ubanks anticipated, but he has his cutoff point: when U.S. heli-copters sweep over Baghdad or on April 15, whichever comes first.

Phil Sands, a twenty-five-year-old from Britain, has been here for more than five weeks, but he's suddenly been ordered out by the Iraqi authorities. They told him, with no explanation, that he was a security risk. In other words, he explains, "They suspect I am a spy." I would give Ubanks that honor. As Sands says good-bye, his backpack and worldly belongings at his feet, he admits he isn't sure he achieved anything: "The war happened. It's still happening. I think a lot of people will get killed, so did I achieve anything? I don't think so."

Seventy-nine-year-old Larita Smith from Jackson, Mississippi, is undoubtedly the oldest shield. She says her family thinks she's crazy, but as an artist, former local reporter, and divorced mother, she's one of those people who has probably never paid much attention to what others think. She marches around in a smock and baggy pants with her camera strung around her neck, hoping to get her stories back to a public-access TV station in Jackson. Asked why she is so opposed to this war, she answers, "Bush's economic program." She figures she might succeed here in getting the attention she failed to muster at home. In her gen-tle drawl, she says, "Down in Mississippi, people need their tax money to live a decent life. Our nursing homes are so crowded and so poor and I'm facing that. You're locked in with a combi-nation lock. You won't get your diaper changed sometimes for twenty-four hours."

She's coughing pretty badly from the sandstorms and the smoke from the oil fires. Given her age and poor health, the Iraqi authorities have let her stay in a hotel and have not forced her to spend the night at one of the human-shield sites. I suspect they've never seen anyone quite like Larita Smith in their lives.

BRENDA BULLETIN: APRIL 2, 2003

Despite what you may have heard, Annie is quite alive and feisty as of this evening. The bomb or missile strike initially reported to have hit the Palestine Hotel actually hit about a football-field length away and was aimed at a building reputedly used by Baath Party functionaries. True, the concussion of the blast was sufficiently unsettling to dump her "unceremoniously" on the floor, but she was otherwise unharmed. She had some uncharacteristically sharp remarks for the wire-service reporter who aired some wildly unfounded reports that were picked up and passed on by CNN, who apparently could not resist adding a few breathless twists of their own. It wasn't until late last evening that everything got put into proper perspective.

It is true that the ground war seems to be moving closer to Baghdad, but if not exactly inured to the cacophony, Annie seems at least to be taking it in stride. There was an amusing interchange this morning when the Washington interviewer, upon hearing a particularly loud explosion in the background, said "Jeeezus, Annie, what was that?" To which she replied, "Oh, THAT really wasn't anything."

I would tell you more about the arrival of the network bimbette in the very tight T-shirt, but perhaps it's better that you have something to look forward to.

V

APRIL 3, 2003

I wake up at 6 a.m. to utter silence. This is the first time in a while that I'm not roused by thuds. The smoke has settled on the horizon, and at last I catch a glimpse of blue sky. Amer calls it the calm before the storm. But it doesn't take long for the Iraqis to stoke the oil fires around the city and get them going again. I had once mistaken the black plumes for the aftermath of bombing, but Amer corrected me, saying bombs produce white smoke. These are like funeral pyres.

The new twist of the day is that under current rules Amer can't be both my translator (with him I can't use the word *minder*) and my driver, so we have had to hire a driver. Who knows why? Perhaps this is a way of adding another layer of costly snitches. Amer, however, has once again found just the right guy. Mohammed is twenty-eight. He is as short and stocky as Amer is long and lean. And while Amer goes for suits, Mohammed remains an overgrown teenager, preferring T-shirts with English phrases on them and baggy pants. At first I thought he actually might be retarded, but it turns out he's just a flake. However, he speaks fluent English, has the right credentials, and isn't going to get in the way. He is the son of the Iraqi ambassador to Austria, a lost soul who clearly did too many drugs at some point in his life. A child of privilege, he went to high school in the United States while his father was posted there. He came back to Iraq, but he doesn't fit in. He isn't a dissident. He's not an intelligence agent, or at least not a serious one. He is just lost. He never did military service, has no college education, and seriously asks me what happened to Jason on *Days of Our Lives*. He is disappointed that I can't fill him in on ten years of soaps. His favorite TV program was *The Cosby Show*. "I guess it's not on anymore," he says wistfully. Then he asks me about the clubs in Washington, D.C., which he clearly frequented all too often.

It's another bus "tour du jour," and like good schoolchildren, we take our seats. As usual we are not told in advance where we're going. As the bus wends its way, seemingly endlessly, through the city, I start to lose it, calling out to officials up front, "Where are we going?" Of course there's no answer. I hate being out of control.

For several blocks near the Republican Palace, shop windows have been shattered by repeated explosions, though the shops themselves remain untouched. Our destination is the Baghdad Trade Fair, which Amer and I visited on our own yesterday. This is not going to add much to what I already know. The place is crawling with Baath Party members, hardly an inducement for people to pour out their innermost feelings. However, I happen on an endearing twelve-year-old boy who is selling candy to support his widowed mother. I ask what he thinks about Americans coming to Baghdad, and without missing a beat he says, "Great." A man listening in quickly intervenes and moves him off.

Amer says this particular neighborhood was once a favorite haunt for Uday, Saddam's elder son. There are stories about him parading the streets with his tiger before he was seriously wounded in an assassination attempt in the mid-'90s. Unable to hide his disgust, Amer says Uday would also prey on local girls. Word has it that to refuse Uday could mean an ugly death.

Back at the Palestine, we have another briefing with Information Minister Mohammed al-Sahaf, whose grip on reality is slipping even more. Dressed in his dapper battle-dress and beret, he sticks to his rosy version. To reporters who gently suggest his accounts are at odds with known American successes, he answers, in effect, that we are hallucinating. Asked about reports that American troops have seized part of Baghdad's main airport and are within sight of the city, he replies with no evident shame that the Americans are not even within 100 miles of Baghdad. This is the world we have to live in. Contradicting him, challenging him head-on, would get us nowhere, except expelled.

A colleague seated next to me hands me a note: "I want what he's smoking." What does he really think he's doing? The more dire the situation, the more he defies reality. He certainly has a captive audience.

It is curious that officials don't mention the Iraqi army as such. They speak of Iraqi defenses being led by the militias of the Baath Party, tribal units, or the Fedayeen Saddam, the black-uniformed thugs who are amongst the most feared of Saddam's forces. Foreign volunteers also come in for a lot of praise. Vice President Ramadan claims that 6,000 Arab volunteers have arrived, with more than half of them ready to act as suicide bombers. He promises we will see the results of this campaign before long.

There are still few signs in the city of preparations for street-to-street fighting, apart from the groups of armed Baath Party members and local militias, most of whom sit in white plastic chairs doing nothing. There are some trucks, covered in mud, hidden among civilian houses under date trees. The Iraqi press, such as it is, and television have not mentioned that anything unusual has happened at the airport, but Iraqis know that American and British troops are approaching. I went to the open-air market today, and as I entered, one of the many merchants selling canned tomatoes had his ear glued to the BBC on a shortwave radio. I asked him what he thought about the news that U.S. and British troops might be as close as twenty miles. He looked up, startled that I'd caught him listening to the Beeb, and said, "Lies, lies, all lies," and then promptly went back to listening.

People continue to be incredibly friendly, which says more than the words they utter. At one stall I am offered a soft drink. Most here are Shiites, and I ask them why the Shiites have not risen up against Saddam as they did in 1991 and as the United States anticipated they would again. They all answer that this war is totally different. Then, they say, the United States was justified in pushing Iraq out of Kuwait. Then, some say, there was hope, a reference to what many think was the betrayal by the United States when it sat back and did nothing to help the insurrectionists.

Sixteen days is a long time in a bombing campaign, and people are exhausted. You can see the strain. A woman comes up to me asking why President Bush is waging war against innocent

people. The more she talks, the more she is racked by sobs. A
friend gently ushers her away.

When we get back in the car, Amer, a Sunni Muslim, says
the Shiites loathe Saddam, whatever they may say to me. He says
Shiites have never forgotten one particular incident. When they
rose up against the regime in the wake of the '91 Gulf War, Saddam's son-in-law Hussein Kamel and his forces damaged the
domed tomb of Hussein, the grandson of the prophet Mohammed, in Karbala—a holy site second only to Mecca in terms
of the number of Shiite pilgrims who visit it. That was bad
enough, but Hussein Kamel dismissed the subsequent outrage,
daring to compare himself to the revered Shiite hero, saying "I
am also Hussein." This man did not know the meaning of hu-
mility. After he defected to Jordan and spilled his guts to the
United States about banned weapons programs, he was disappointed with his reception and decided he would be better off
back in Baghdad. On his return, Saddam had him assassinated.

At 8 p.m. the lights suddenly go out. No large explosion pre-
ceded the blackout, so it is unclear who or what caused it. The
entire city is plunged into darkness. I have my trusty headlamp,
courtesy of a wilderness outfitter. This is one good result of love-
enforced camping with Vint in Montana as well as my time in
Afghanistan. If not for those times, I would never know about
this incredibly useful item. My hands are free, and I can see and
type at the same time. I wander out into the hallway for a reality
check just as Amer arrives to make sure I am managing all right.
I give him a spare headlamp. He's balked in the past every time I
have asked him if he is all right, as if it were unseemly to ask
that. At last I can do something useful for this man who has done
so much for me.

It takes forever to get through on the satellite phone. I finish
the piece for ATC and broadcast with the roar of the hotel generator in the background. It only provides a dim light in the hall-

way, but for now the elevators are still working. I collapse at
1 a.m. from dialing fatigue.

BRENDA BULLETIN: APRIL 3, 2003

Getting on toward crunch time. Lights now out in the city. Her
satellite-phone batteries will only last a couple of hours without
recharge. In the information vacuum, her editor promises to relay
anything he hears. Long talk with her, which may be the last time we
will talk like that for a bit.

Ironic that as big things crumble, small bureaucratic machines
grind on. Yesterday, what is left of the press corps lined up like mis-
creant school children to get their new press ID cards, turning in the
old pink ones for new yellow ones. Annie wondered if the star
comes next. There was a scurrying around for photos. Annie finally
found one taken of her in Kosovo. Amer said it made her look like a
"monster." The fellow has such a way with words sometimes. But
she has learned there is a strict photographic protocol among Iraqis
to always look one's best before the camera, no matter what the
occasion.

The press corps yet again had to settle past accounts with the
Ministry of Information just for the pleasure of being there. *News-
week* got socked for $15,000, little NPR for $1,500. Tempers flared
in the long queue. An arrogant French journalist, feeling entitled,
tried to barge in ahead of Annie, saying, "I am French, you are
nothing!" Annie briefly became Brenda and stomped on the delicate
Froggy femme's foot and sent her reeling. So much for politesse and
camaraderie.

The Palestine is rife with rumor and intrigue. The grizzled reporter for *The New York Times*, John Burns, may be kicked out at
last. On hearing this, Annie's editor asked her if she wanted to grab
a seat in the Burns Exit Convoy. She contemplated twelve hours of

being cooped up with Burns's vitriolic fury and opted to stay put. There is some question if they can even get out at this point, and anyway she wants to stay. At last read some sort of face-saving accommodation had been reached. Burns, perhaps marginally muzzled, is to stay. There are at least two TV crews—one French, one Italian—who have been detained in the hotel since the beginning. Prohibited from reporting, they have no permission to leave. That sounds like the worst of fates.

Annie remains well stocked with fresh fruit, thanks to Amer. Produce is trickling in if you know where to find it, and he does. The alcoholic stocks are also holding up, and should they run low, there is again available a particularly virulent brand of local firewater called Iraq Arak for a buck a bottle. Perhaps if she mixed this with Cheer-Up she could come up with something approximating what my delightful bartending first-cousin-once-removed calls a "Slow Screw Against the Wall."

Her biggest problem in the early a.m. today was that she desperately needed some toenail clippers. My guess is that she has bigger troubles on her plate now.

Wish her well.

V

APRIL 4, 2003

Cold water, but at least there is still water, albeit sporadic, and I top up my garbage pails so I have reserves in case the taps shut down altogether. There is no light in the bathroom—and no window—so ablutions are performed in the dark. Probably just as well. Thank god I got some laundry done yesterday, because who knows when the opportunity will arise again.

The room is now even more like a cave, but the narrow glass doors onto the balcony are a comfort because there is not much of them to shatter. Unfortunately this also means there is almost no daylight. I keep thinking I should move the beds around to make the room more secure. Jon Lee Anderson and Paul Mc-Geough have transformed their room into a snug bunker by turning the bed frames on their sides as a barrier against incoming fire. They sleep on mattresses on the floor surrounded by their protective wall.

The lack of electricity has plunged Iraqis into new despair. Everyone is in the dark now, literally and figuratively. Though Iraqis lived for months in '91 without electricity, they thought this time would be different. They believed that the United States would not target the infrastructure and convinced themselves this war would be easier. Indeed they have high, perhaps overly high, expectations of how precise the bombing will be. Now they don't know what to expect and, more poignantly, they don't know what to expect from one another. They have lived in fear for so long that there is no trust even among family members.

Virtually no one is venturing out into the streets at night, and not many do so during the day. Aid officials say that, unlike in '91, a crucial water-pumping station about twenty miles north of the city is equipped with generators, some of them provided by the Red Cross for just such a crisis. But water and sewage plants are on the outskirts, so it may be impossible for employees to reach and service them if fighting on the ground gets really bad. After so many years of sanctions, these installations are working way below capacity, repaired with little more than Scotch tape when they should have long ago been replaced.

My computer and sat-phone batteries run out quickly, so I have to hole up in Amer's car to recharge them from the lighter socket. But I have a car battery in reserve just in case. We lug it up the stairs (the elevator goes out for a while). Those things are heavy! I hook up some jumper cables to a portable AC/DC converter, plug in my equipment, and bingo, everything is working. Experience from Afghanistan yet again comes into play. Some other reporters, who are more organized and flush than I, have small generators in their rooms. (Given how much I am smoking I think it just as well I don't have one, with all the attendant cans of diesel.) They promise I can use their generators if my battery contraption fails.

What staff there is left in the hotel is really stressed. I haven't seen anyone on the floor today and guess there won't be clean sheets for a long time to come. I can't make coffee in the room anymore—the car battery can't handle the kettle—so I have to go downstairs, where the coffee shop is brewing something on propane burners. The restaurant, which was never good, has reached an all-time low. Despite dinner hours slated to start at 8:30, the doors now don't open until well after 9 and the cook is extremely grouchy because he has no help. And surprise, surprise it's the same awful meal we have had for ten days. I haven't eaten in a couple of days again and am getting jittery. Amer goes out in search of some edible takeout.

While he is out, Amer checks in on friends in the southwest suburbs. He sees people fleeing into the city from the airport area while others try to leave the city altogether. Residents have been told to abandon three neighborhoods because the Republican Guard and Fedayeen Saddam are to take up positions there. At least, in this instance, they are getting a warning, since most of the time Iraqi troops just move in unannounced and use civilians for cover.

Amer's friends in the nearby suburb of Huriya expect they will be ordered out next. Just a week ago this family was defiant, saying they would take up arms and fight the Americans in the streets if need be. Now they say Iraq doesn't have a chance, and given the inevitability of defeat, they want Saddam to step down, leave the country, and spare his people.

These are the first real signs, after a brief moment of defiance, that people see the end in sight. Even a statement read in the name of Saddam seems to hint at the first signs of official anxiety, and even disappointment with Iraqi military units. It says that anyone who is unable to fight must withdraw and give an opportunity to someone else. The statement also calls on Baath Party members to stay true to their oath. Tonight there was footage of someone said to be Saddam visiting residential areas of Baghdad. If indeed it was he, this would be his first public appearance in two years. But what is amazing is that he is doing nothing, at least nothing visible, to help his people. He doesn't visit the wounded, or the troops. This is all just fiddling while Rome burns, a delaying action with the end now clear.

I swear I heard artillery today. Whether this came from jumpy Iraqi soldiers shooting wildly in the air or from American troops who may have reached the city, no one knows.

It's Friday, the Muslim holy day, and many people go to the mosques, where they look not only for solace but for information. Journalists follow. The Abu Hanifa an-Nu'man mosque in the al-Adhamiya district is crowded to overflowing. During the sermon the imam, Abdul Ghafour al-Qasi, tells the faithful the powerful Iraqi forces were able to defeat the Americans at the airport. He urges the congregation not to listen "to the aggressors' media."

Meanwhile, the ineffable Information Minister Mohammed al-Sahaf continues his daily show with increasing glee. His demonic laughter reached new heights today. Comparing British and American forces to a "snake in a quagmire," he relishes his newest appellation, "lost desert animals"—but like the imam's, his description of the war is increasingly at odds with U.S. and British reports from the battlefield, a fact that is not lost on more and more Iraqis. Today he said American troops, tanks and all, had been air-dropped into the airport, an interesting concept. Clearly he did not wish to acknowledge, however absurd his explanations, that the Americans had managed to enter over land. That would have contradicted his portrayal of American troops "nailed in Umm Qasr, Nasiriya, Najaf, and Kut."

He makes an ominous pledge at today's follies. Promising "nonconventional action" against U.S.-led forces at the airport, he says, "This is not military. We will do something to them that will be a great example for those mercenaries." At the words "nonconventional," a ripple goes through the press corps. Is this an admission that the Iraqis would use chemical weapons? "No," he says, explaining that Iraqis might resort to martyrdom or guerrilla actions, adding, "We will do something which I believe is very beautiful, very new and creative."

APRIL 5, 2003

Amer appears with his mustache much reduced in size. He found a barber who was still open and he managed to get a hot shave. He's a little put out, though, by the excessive mustache trim. It was his pride and joy. It always strikes me how banal war is on a day-to-day basis, and how ordinary things remain important. In *Berlin Diaries*, one of the great books about World War Two, author Marie Vassiltchikov spends much of the devastating bombing looking for a pretty hat. In Bosnia, where there was a critical shortage of medicines, friends would nonetheless put luxurious face creams at the top of their wish lists, explaining that they just needed something to make them "feel like a human being." In Kosovo the local women remained coifed, made up, and neatly dressed amidst the terror.

Here at the Palestine, the hotel generator provides enough power for one dim light over the bed. That's it. In desperation, I figure out how to hotwire this light to an electrical strip, so now

I have power for the computer and the satellite phone. A vast improvement as the car battery only lasted for about twelve hours before I had to recharge it, and that meant humping it down eleven flights, putting it in Amer's car for a couple of hours, and then humping it back up eleven flights. Amer was jealous of my Rube Goldberg technique, but he was too proud to have me, a mere woman, come and rewire his room. Instead he got an electrician to come in and, it's true, he now has much better power than I. His TV and refrigerator even work! But he can have the TV. I don't speak Arabic, but after days of enforced practice I can sing the songs to Saddam, including the new ones that are being produced. I just worry that the hotel generator will become so overloaded with our creative rewiring that it will simply explode, leaving us in total darkness.

Early this morning, rumors began to spread through this sprawling city of five million that American troops had indeed finally entered Baghdad. I got online and checked the wires and, yup, Abrams tanks and Bradley fighting vehicles from the Army's 3rd Infantry Division entered Baghdad in broad daylight today. They came up from the south, turned left at the Tigris, and then headed for the newly renamed Baghdad International Airport, which has been under U.S. control since yesterday.

I'd personally seen no signs of American troops in the city center, and with phone service now out, limiting communications around town, they were initially hard to pinpoint, but Amer tripped on them when he tried to drive out to the southern edge of the city. Qadm was apparently desperate to find out if his wife and children are safe, given that American troops have come up through the villages where they are staying with relatives. He asked Amer to take him south, in the direction of Babylon. They were blocked as they tried to leave the city and saw the remains of the first U.S. probe. Four-wheel-drive Nissans, the vehicle of choice for senior Iraqi officials, smoldered on the highway. Destroyed Iraqi military vehicles and the remnants of heavy artillery, rocket launchers, and antiaircraft guns littered the road. Among the detritus of what had clearly been a fierce fight was an American tank.

I persuaded Amer to take me back there so I could check it out. I didn't dare get out of the car because Iraqi troops were still in the area, but I confirmed the damage, and the carnage. The corpses of dozens of Iraqi soldiers could be seen along the highway.

Since the roads are blocked from the south, Iraqis now have to ditch their cars and walk into Baghdad. A man who reached the city said with astonishment that he had seen more than two dozen American military vehicles and hundreds of American troops pass him on the road. The drivers at the hotel are also a great source of information. One of their wives watched as American tanks passed under her window. She wept with relief, not at the sight of American troops, but because they didn't harm her neighborhood.

In districts to the southwest near the airport, Amer tells me, women and children have fled. Only men are left. But if this was supposed to be a valiant stand by the Republican Guard, it has fizzled. According to a friend of Amer's, six members of that elite force retreated from the airport area, running across open fields to his house. They said many in their unit had been killed or had surrendered. This friend was in despair at how quickly the Iraqi forces had folded, telling Amer, "We have lost."

Meanwhile, Information Minister al-Sahaf remains defiant to the point of absurdity, telling us the Iraqis have ousted the Americans from the airport. He tells us we are free to go and see for ourselves. In fact, we are not. Once he has left, other officials from the Ministry of Information tell us that not only are we not allowed in the southern surburb of Dora, but we would be crazy to go there because it is too dangerous. (Sahaf also promised us a victorious tour of the airport within the hour. Needless to say, it didn't happen.)

BRENDA BULLETIN: APRIL 5, 2003

Annie is now asleep after a chaotic day in which she and the intrepid Amer got places (she said "I'll tell you how later") that no other journalist did. First into the southern part of the city, where the U.S. armor burst through in its lightning foray; then out near the airport, where sporadic resistance continues; then into forbidden neighborhoods; and finally into civilian hospitals, which were in fact filled with wounded, cowering Republican Guards. She was interviewing one man who said that he was just a simple civilian, sitting at home minding his business, when his house was hit by dastardly Americans. The patient's father, however, not hearing this story, then blew the poor fellow's cover by proudly boasting that his son was an Iraqi and could endure pain—he was after all an officer in the Republican Guard. It was then established that this young man had, yes, been in his house when it was hit, but he was with his commander and other officers.

Confusion and chaos reign. People who last week were promising to fight to the bitter end are fleeing, saying that all is lost. Annie called just before tucking up, dirty and very tired. Still no electricity at the Palestine; water cold and dirty; wine levels down and the still-unopened bottle of gin looking like an option. "I look like I've been in garden muck all day," she says. Annie loves muck of any kind. Her hair, now embedded with a crust of Iraqi sand, is no longer brushed but molded. Drawing on the past, she calls it "Afghan hairspray."

I ask her if she wants to see what I have been writing about her. She has been off the Brenda List for almost a month. Maybe it will be a diversion, maybe give her a laugh. She's too tired to say no. Her editor called shortly thereafter. "She's something else," he said with relief and something of an appreciative laugh. "She's been very naughty today, your girl, but she scooped everyone. Extraordinary stuff." I guess Annie did not exactly check in with the boss to get permission.

V

APRIL 6, 2003

Vint sent me a bunch of Brenda Bulletins. He had taken me off the list lest I know how worried he's been, but after we talked he realized we both knew, but weren't telling each other, about all the possible scenarios. I am overwhelmed, and not a little daunted by his extraordinary prose. He's supposed to be the artist in the family! A friend has called them "love letters," and indeed that is what they are.

This is all much easier on me than on him. I just lurch from day to day, desperately making sure I have something to file morning, noon, and night. I honestly don't have time to be frightened most of the time, and when there is a lull, I just fall asleep. And I sleep so soundly that in the morning I have to check with my fellow reporters to find out if there was bombing overnight. How embarrassing to admit that I slept through much of "Shock and Awe." But frankly the bombing hasn't been very bad, and it is stunningly accurate for the most part. I don't know what lies ahead, though.

While I do a two-way for *Weekend Sunday* with Liane Hansen, the bombs finally let loose with a radio-worthy racket while I am on the air. For some reason every time I have broadcast before, they have fallen silent. Today they really shook me and the hotel.

The Information Ministry now wants us to go to Dora, so the tour du jour is what Amer and I saw on our own yesterday—the burned-out American tank. Today there is a large crater next to it. It looks like the Americans came back to put it well and truly out of commission so the Iraqis could not use it. Iraqi kids and soldiers clamber over it, posing for the cameras, but as war planes roar overhead they run for cover, as do I. I'm not wearing my bulletproof vest or helmet. Now that ground fire is more likely I guess I had better, but it is so heavy I can barely move in it. If I tilt to one side I topple over.

Iraqi officials claim there are several other destroyed American tanks, but provide no evidence to support this, and when the Information Minister does his stand-up comedy routine today, repeating assertions that the Iraqis have beaten the Americans back from the airport, I catch some officials looking pretty despondent, maybe even angry at his lies. As to how the Americans could be seen at the airport if they were not indeed there, Sahaf has another creative answer: they were using stage sets. Disney meets Baghdad.

Masses of people are trying to leave the city. The roads north and east are bumper-to-bumper. It's hard to imagine there's anyone left here. There are long lines around gas stations, but many acknowledge it's now probably too late.

Amer and I discuss possible story ideas. He has described to me how Iraqis remain tied to their clans, which are subsets of the larger tribes that divide Iraqis. Even though he left his hometown of Ramadi long ago for Baghdad, Amer continues to donate what he can each month to the clan, which is a large, extended family grouping numbering in the hundreds. The money goes for weddings, funerals, and the needy.

I would like to meet a tribal sheikh, or clan leader, but given the atmosphere of fear, Amer suggests we wait because now, as he rightly says, I won't hear anything approximating people's real feelings. He has close friends in the al-Mashadani tribe, one of the most important in Iraq. Though they are based in al-Tarmia, just fifty kilometers north of Baghdad, there is no way, given current conditions, for us to get there. Their story, as he tells it, is a microcosm of Iraq under Saddam.

Saddam's half brother Sabawi appropriated some of the best Mashadani tribal land. While defending the rich pasture, one of the sheikh's sons was shot and killed. Members of the tribe took revenge, shooting up Sabawi's house. The sheikh's other sons were then arrested and ordered to be executed. A meeting between Saddam and the tribal leaders was called to resolve the brewing crisis. This was by no means the first time one of Saddam's half brothers had caused problems but, despite internal family feuds, Saddam relied on them and tolerated their excesses.

The sheikh told Saddam, "We are at your mercy," but he also added, "We have defended you and sacrificed our men in many wars, and we are loyal members of the Republican Guard." It was a veiled threat. Saddam was caught between the demands of his family and tribal politics. He agreed to release the sheikh's sons, but he refused to return the land. It ended in an uneasy standoff that is still being played out behind the scenes. Amer suggests that this is just one of many reasons the Republican Guard has failed to fight as expected, and he thinks that these family and tribal disputes will continue long into the future.

At about 10 p.m. Tim in the next-door room knocks, just to make sure I am OK. I really don't know him very well and am very touched.

APRIL 7, 2003

All night there has been the sound of fighting, but for the first time I can clearly hear machine guns. Something is going on right across the river. I stand on the balcony in my nightie looking out across the muddy-green Tigris to the palaces, ministries, and security headquarters that have symbolized Saddam's power. I struggle to identify what appear to be four military vehicles coming around a bend of the Tigris. They approach the Republican Palace. There is an exchange of gunfire. Tim, the ITN cameraman on the next balcony, says they are American Bradleys. An ammunition dump explodes in front of us. Iraqi troops flee their trenches and run for the river, some still in their underwear. Two raise their hands and give themselves up. It looks like they were ordered to lie facedown on the ground. The clouds move in, blocking the view. As Tim's videotape later shows, one of the Iraqi soldiers turns over. An American soldier shoots him. The body convulses and then lies motionless.

Far from seeming liberated, Baghdad feels claustrophobic. All day long the sound of rockets, antiaircraft guns, and artillery presses in from all directions. The fog of sand and smoke from the fires envelopes the city. Drivers who dare to venture out can't see what's going on just a few yards down the road. Families have no idea how relatives and friends are faring because the phone lines remain cut.

An American plane has dropped four 2,000-pound bombs in Mansour, an exclusive Baghdad neighborhood, apparently following a tip that a senior leadership meeting was happening there. When we get to the site, there's nothing but rubble and no sign that Saddam is under it. There's no evidence of unusual security activity.

The information minister hurried to the hotel to repeat assurances that American troops were in headlong flight and had failed to penetrate the city. Little matter that gunfire rages just a few hundred yards away. Be assured, he said. Baghdad is safe, secure, and victorious.

The largely deserted streets and constant sound of small arms and mortars testify to a different reality. To the north of the river, which divides Baghdad, soldiers who'd been manning trenches disappear. A quick bus tour organized by the Information Ministry is designed to show us that there are no American troops in the city, and we see none. It's a quick tour. Perhaps the driver was scared.

Iraqis answer questions with questions: "What's going on?" "Do you know where the Americans are?" "How long will this go on?" "How long do you think the Americans will stay?"—an admission that they will be here, even if the good minister says they aren't already. There is weariness and wariness. Those who dare to admit they loathe Saddam voice suspicion about American promises of liberation. They hear reports that the United States might stay in Iraq for years. They say they don't want to be ruled by a foreign power.

As I wrap up the day, Amer calls from his room with an interesting tidbit. Iraqi TV made no mention of the anniversary of the founding of the Baath Party. It's usually a major holiday but today: nothing.

APRIL 8, 2003

The battle for the center of Baghdad begins before dawn within the sprawling gardens of Saddam Hussein's Republican Palace. The fighting takes place behind a curtain of date trees, but I can track the progress by watching the tracers, smoke, and flares gradually shift as American tanks repel an Iraqi assault. The tanks then move out of the palace compound into the city's open streets. Eventually two tanks move onto and hold one of the main bridges spanning the river. For more than seven hours the palace grounds resound with artillery, rockets, mortars, and tank guns backed by the vicious strafing of an A-10 Warthog. The plane moves slowly above the hotel and then lets rip on the Planning Ministry with volleys of cannon rounds—they turn the building into flaming Swiss cheese. The noise is like nothing I've ever heard. I record it, but when I listen later, the result doesn't even begin to capture the reality. It reminds me of Chechnya, when I dutifully hauled out my microphone and recorded the ferocious, and utterly indiscriminate carpet bombing the Russians unleashed—all the while lying in a snowy ditch shaking uncontrollably. When I filed the tape, a producer back in Washington took it out of the piece, with the cutting comment, "You know, it really sounds like a car backfiring." He was right, but I wished he could have left me believing it had somehow been worth the effort.

While waiting to do a two-way for *Morning Edition*, my editor, Doug Roberts, keeps me up to date. He tells me that a correspondent from Al Jazeera has just been wounded. Then he tells me the man has died. He was caught in the morning's battle while broadcasting from the roof of their office building. As I get off the phone, there's a huge blast that literally throws me from my chair. The hotel shudders. I think another bomb has landed close by and continue typing. The hotel phone rings. It's Amer. I assume he wants to tell me about an upcoming press conference and I start to mutter that I'm about to go on the air when he interrupts with the words "Get out now. Hotel hit." I am struck by a rush of adrenaline and a surreal calm all at once. I have been anticipating something like this for too many days. I go straight for the sat phone. If the hotel is going up in flames I figure I'd better take the phone with me. I struggle to unplug and disentangle all the cables, and in my rush I trip over an extension cord, yanking my laptop off the desk. There's a sickening crash as it hits the floor. "So I'll have to write my scripts by hand from now on," I think as I dash out the door. I stuff the various parts of the sat phone into a backpack—hiding the sat phone is now instinct—and hurtle down the eleven flights of stairs along with lots of other panicked reporters.

The lobby is full of people. I can't find Amer. It turns out he had run up another staircase to make sure I had gotten out. He finally appears, out of breath. First there's relief that there doesn't seem to be much damage. There's no sign of any fire. Someone points to a chipped balcony on the 15th floor, four floors above my room. It doesn't look very bad. But then the casualties appear. Someone wrapped in a bloody sheet is carried out. Then another body. Everyone is desperately asking one another who's been hurt. The photographers and camera crews crowd around, making it difficult to get the injured into waiting cars. We aren't even thoughtful about our own.

Most of us immediately assumed an Iraqi irregular, angered by Iraqi setbacks in the war and knowing the hotel housed foreign journalists, had taken a potshot at the building with a shoulder-launched, rocket-propelled grenade. However, a television camera had recorded the turn of a U.S. tank turret, its aim at the hotel, and the subsequent blast. News comes from the hospital: two cameramen have died. Three others remain in the hospital with wounds.

The shell glanced off the balcony, spraying those standing in room 1502 with concrete and metal. There's a pool of blood, and an overturned camera still lying on the floor where one of the cameramen fell. Colleagues stand around, shaken. Some are weeping. Seamus Conlan, a photographer for World Picture News, says, "I don't know how many people you know personally who have been killed in this work, but I know a lot."

And it could easily have been he who was killed today. Just a few hours earlier, at dawn, he had been fired on by American troops while he was taking pictures from the roof of the hotel. Conlan said he first saw a tracer bullet flash over his head and then immediately afterward heard the whistling of several other bullets close by. He slid down the roof and hid behind a ledge for cover.

At an early briefing at Central Command HQ in Qatar, Brigadier General Vincent Brooks initially says the hotel was targeted after soldiers were fired on from the lobby, which would have been a physical impossibility. Later he tells reporters, "I may have misspoken." U.S. military officials then say a tank from the 3rd Infantry had fired on the hotel, after reporting that "significant" enemy fire had come from a position in front of the eighteen-story hotel. The Commander of the 3rd Infantry Division's 2nd Brigade, which deployed the tank, eventually reports that the crew aimed at the Palestine after seeing enemy "binoculars." This was the dozens of lenses of TV and still cameras that were trained on the battle. I have to go on the air, but first I call Vint to let him know I am not one of the victims.

I can barely contain my anger, and the explanations coming out of Central Command in Doha do nothing to improve the situation. No one at the hotel saw or heard any outgoing fire. A spokesman says the soldiers didn't know the building they were aiming at was the Palestine, despite its distinctive architecture, and the well-known fact that just about every journalist in town is living and working here. For nearly three weeks, foreign reporters have operated with the gnawing fear that a so-called smart bomb or missile might inadvertently slam into our temporary home. It really didn't occur to anyone that the hotel in central Baghdad would be deliberately targeted by U.S. ground forces.

And I am furious with Al Jazeera for putting its people in unnecessary danger. While most of us have had to live and work at the Palestine under the scrutiny of the Information Ministry, Qatar-based Al Jazeera was permitted to have its own headquarters and its own exclusive camera position. Its building, just across the river, was near the Republican Palace and Information Ministry. When the bombing started Al Jazeera had informed U.S. forces about its precise location, but the staff continued to work there even when the area was surrounded by Republican Guard and Fedayeen and was clearly going to be right smack in the middle of the battle zone. To say, as one al Jazeera staffer did, that this was just a residential area is rubbish. This particular tragedy was avoidable.

The toll on Iraqis also appears to be severe. Amer and I go around to hospitals, where the wounded are pouring in by ambulance, taxi, private car, even on foot. Many of the hospitals won't let us in, presumably because they are overwhelmed with military casualties. At the al-Kindi hospital, the emergency room is covered in blood. Many of the wounded are men in uniform, though the head doctor, clearly under orders, insists they are civilians. Asked how many people have been treated, the staff says they have long since stopped counting.

There are also many injured civilians. Many have been caught in the crossfire. Some were in their cars when the tanks appeared and they were fired at, their vehicles turned to toast. While I was there a father carried in his four-year-old son. He was pronounced dead on arrival. His twelve-year-old daughter was also killed when the modest carpentry shop the family called home was hit. His wife lay on a gurney. Her beige sundress was soaked in blood from the waist down. A doctor said she too would die and left to treat someone else. The hospital is understaffed as doctors and nurses can't make it to work because of the fighting. In the hospital morgue there are already fifteen corpses dumped in a walk-in refrigerator, among them the body of the Al Jazeera correspondent, still wearing his flak jacket.

The death toll for journalists in this short war has been high, and as always it comes in ways you don't or can't anticipate. At the Palestine we survived the worst of the bombing to be hit by an American tank shell in broad daylight. Others, traveling with U.S. troops, have been killed in car accidents or by friendly fire. A British correspondent fell off a roof. A total of nine have died during the first three weeks, falling victim to Iraqi or U.S. fire, land mines, or suicide bombings. Four others have died in accidents or through illness.

I remember talking to Kurt Schork, a veteran Reuters reporter, in Kosovo a few years ago. We both said it was time to start winding down this war business. We chatted about what we would do next. He was subsequently killed in Sierra Leone, an assignment I turned down. I know I don't understand Africa and have no instinct about how to survive there. Is my luck running out?

While Baghdad has been the highest-profile assignment I've had, it has not been the scariest, despite all the concerns of friends, family, and NPR listeners. As I think back, the days after reporter Danny Pearl was abducted and subsequently executed in Pakistan may have been the worst. There wasn't a war, but the threats from unknown people against all the other American journalists remaining in Pakistan were haunting.

Like Danny Pearl, I had been trying to follow up on the fate of the radical Islamic groups that Pakistani President Pervez Musharraf had finally banned at the urging of the United States. I wanted to find out how they were responding to the new restrictions after years of being supported and nurtured by the Pakistani security services. While Danny was following up on specific leads to specific people, I was on a fishing expedition. I just "dropped in" on those I could find, who had gone underground. They had no time to prepare the elaborate kidnapping that was Danny's fate.

The day he disappeared I was back, alone, in the house NPR had rented in Islamabad. My boss Loren Jenkins called to say that *The New York Times* and others were moving their reporters into the Marriott hotel for security reasons. I understood their thinking. These were high-profile organizations at risk, but I also had misgivings about going to the high-profile hotel, where reporters could be easily found and identified. My misgivings were quickly confirmed when a Pakistani newspaper published an article that viciously went after a broadcast by CBS for reporting that Osama bin Laden had been in a Rawalpindi hospital shortly before the attack on the World Trade Center. It proceeded to list the room numbers of the CBS staffers in the Marriott, which was little more than an invitation to murder. I felt comfortable in our modest house, where I could just hunker down in anonymity. That night, though, the wind picked up, rattling the shutters. Then the phone started ringing. When I answered it, there was no one at the other end. This happened several times over several hours. What I felt that night was terror, raw terror.

E-mails from listeners often raise the question of why I do what I do. "It is infinitely fascinating" is the crude answer, but I am really not very interested in the strictly military part of war. Rather I am fascinated by how people survive, and how the process of war affects the attitudes of all sides involved, and how they pull out of it.

By nightfall, the areas held by the Americans have fallen silent, suggesting that much of the Iraqi resistance has died away. It is strange to think my NPR colleague Eric Westervelt, who is embedded with an army unit, is just a couple of miles from here. It is still too dangerous for us to try to meet. So close, but still a world away.

BRENDA BULLETIN: APRIL 8, 2003

I hope those of you who have harbored doubts about our Batty Babe's grasp of military nomenclature heard her report this morning, peppered with an impressive array of technological military jargon. Brenda described in detail the seven-hour battle that took place literally before her as she watched from the balcony of her 11th-floor room at the Palestine Hotel. True, she had some help from a former Rhodesian soldier manning a TV camera next door. Tim gave her a primer on the identification of ordnance songs. Some of us do warblers, others do howitzers. It is unsettling to hear this most unmilitary of human beings go into considerable depth on the capabilities of the Gatling cannon in the nose of a Warthog. These aircraft don't actually hover, but they can fly extremely slowly and when they let loose, she said, it sounds like something primordial in heat. She had a mezzanine seat throughout. Smartly, she and Tim had decided that the last place they wanted to be was on the 18th-floor roof, where others journalists raced and goggled for a better view. What happened next is still unclear.

In any case, some poor sod manning a tank cannon in the American column looked across the river and saw all the cavorting journos peering at them through binoculars and fired off a round. Five were hit—one Ukrainian fellow and a Spanish cameraman later died. The wounded had to be carried down fifteen floors to waiting vans. The feeding frenzy was such among the surviving journalists clustered about the vehicles documenting the fate of their fallen colleagues that the doors of the vans could not be opened. Annie, donning her EMT hat, waded in throwing people aside—to get the vans loaded and off.

If you get the impression that her view of her profession can at times be jaundiced, you are right. The story about her Al Jazeera colleagues illustrates the point. They had maintained a work station in a building very close to the Ministry of Information and various other intelligence installations on the other side of the river. From that vantage point they had far superior camera angles than those at the Palestine. Despite the fact that they were clearly in harm's way and, it's rumored, had asked permission to leave, the working stiffs were prohibited from moving by higher-ups anxious to maintain their pretty pictures. The one reporter that is known to have been killed had worked with NPR in the past.

On a more personal level, Amer's family (wife and three kids) have returned to Baghdad from a village where they had been staying with relatives. Apparently, accommodations were too tight. His neighborhood is still dangerous, so he put everyone in an apartment across the street from the Palestine. Since he would be leaving the hotel to join them, he asked Annie if he had to pay the bill, noting that "the Americans are going to own this place anyway in a couple of days." They decided to play this out straight and the bill was paid. But she has drawn the line here, saying that she will not pony up to the Ministry of Information if they try to exact another fee just for the pleasure of being in Saddam's Iraq.

However, today's nearby battle has terrified Amer's wife and young kids, and he has moved them again to stay with another relative, somewhere, he hopes, that will be quieter. Amer, as you may have gathered, is very special man who, for Annie's sake, has been the right person in the right place and at the right time. Besides providing a vital ear into the regime, he continues to magically provide her one good hot meal a day.

The Palestine basically is nothing more than a shell at this point. The staff, for the most part, has fled. The food, when you can get it, is inedible. The water is cold and dark brown. But our resourceful correspondent has displayed mind-boggling electrical genius. She stripped the wire of the overhead bulb and hotwired the panel to it. Now when the generator runs, she can run her laptop, talk on the sat phone, AND once again heat up water for coffee. She is trying to figure out a way to use her helmet as a wok. Now, that is what I call living.

The other thing that you need to know, and this warms the very cockles of my heart, is that at this point virtually everything she has—laptop, satellite phone, clothing, luggage, and God-knows-what-else—is held together by duct tape.

Lastly, I am sad to report that the recently arrived network bimbette has already lost her digital camera. There is a big sign in the lobby to this effect. If any of you knows where it is, please do tell.

V

APRIL 9, 2003

Silence is much noisier than the boom, boom of bombs. And that's what woke me today. The security guy in the hallway was gone. I walked downstairs into the lobby at about 7. It was empty, completely empty. All the people we have feared for so long have gone, evaporated. The Information Ministry office is locked up.

But it turns out that Uday al-Tae did what Saddam's agents have done so well—using his last shreds of power, he went around extorting money late last night. He never seemed to focus on me, which didn't help when I was trying to wheedle a visa out of him but maybe helped in the end. I still have my cash.

Uday has since disappeared. Qadm has also disappeared. Now I realize why he wouldn't tell me where he lived. Amer confirms that he was in fact an intelligence officer, but as Amer puts it, he was a decent man nonetheless. As intelligence agents go, he was pretty straight. I am sure that he used his charm to get information, but he helped us more than others and he could be disarmingly honest at moments—or was he just very clever? In recent weeks he distanced himself from me, saying one day that he had to be careful as he was perceived to be too pro-American. Heather Abbott from CBC and I had asked how we could contact him if and when chaos broke out and the phones went down. Since addresses are less than useless in Baghdad, I asked him to draw a map of where he lived. He declined. I wonder if we will ever see him again and what he will do. Perhaps he got a cut of the fees we all paid and is living happily in Syria.

One of his underlings—Mr. Mohsen—dared to appear this morning. Greed overcame good sense. His sights were set on the property of a group of Italian journalists who had driven into southern Iraq after the war began. They were captured and subsequently held under guard in the Palestine Hotel along with the French TV crew. Mohsen kept the keys to their vehicles. Early this morning, with marines just a couple of miles from the hotel, Mohsen was caught trying to drive off in the confiscated Mitsubishi. An Italian journalist managed to slash the tires before he could escape. Mohsen begged for mercy and one of the Iraqi drivers finally gave him a lift home. Amer says he was last seen tearing up his Ministry ID card, tossing the fragments out the window.

If there is to be a last-ditch fight by the Republican Guard, Saddam's vaunted troops, or by fanatical irregular forces, they are nowhere to be seen today. In neighborhood after neighborhood the Baath Party members, steely-eyed security, and police have vanished. Iraqi troops have fled their sandbagged trenches. Under a bridge I saw surface-to-air missiles left unmanned. An army jacket and a pair of military boots lay strewn across an intersection. No one knew the fate of Saddam, but suddenly it didn't matter.

Reporters looking for U.S. troops tripped on them in the eastern suburbs, where they found themselves face to face with Abrams tanks. Marines moved quickly into abandoned Iraqi

bunkers. Told there were no Iraqi military units anywhere between them and the city center, the Marine company commander reportedly chortled, "Love it, love it."

What has followed has been an orgy of looting. First there
were just a few clusters of young men on the streets, but as people realized there was nothing stopping them anymore, the
crowds grew, their fury focused on the symbols of Saddam's
power. Groups broke into government buildings and ware-
houses, taking everything that wasn't nailed down and then
some: chairs, air conditioners, computers, even doors. I see a
yacht being pulled along downtown Sadoun Street. Vehicles are
stolen from government parking lots. Amer points to people
pulling or pushing cars because they can't get them started. He
watches all this with growing distress. He is devastated at the
damage.

Defense Secretary Donald Rumsfeld says we are watching
history, the unfolding events that will shape the fate of a people
and potentially the future of the region, but it doesn't look good
from here. Government buildings across the city are on fire. We
pass the Olympic headquarters, which looters have set ablaze.
This building symbolizes the sick brutality of Saddam and his
family, for it was here that his elder son Uday tortured disap-
pointing athletes or those who merely displeased him. Outside
the Oil Ministry, a young man stands in front of a statue of Saddam imitating his grand gesture. A friend snaps a photo. Such a
lark would have cost him his life just yesterday.

Amer and I stop on a bridge as a column of Marines approach on the highway underneath. I jump out of the car and
lean over the balustrade. I can almost touch the kids sitting on
top of their tanks. Before I can stop myself, I shout down at
them, "Hey, guys!" One turns around with an M16 pointed at
me. I raise my hands and hear myself screaming "No! No! I'm
an American." For so many days I had felt the bombs, or seen

the tanks. Suddenly, I am face-to-face with American troops and peering down a muzzle. I hadn't realized how threatened I felt by the recent days' events and how relieved I was that the Americans are finally here, and also how relieved I am to think that this phase of the war might be over soon. Just last week it seemed the war could go on for weeks if not months, and I was having trouble imagining how I would last.

Another column of Marines moves through Saddam City, the poor, predominantly Shiite Muslim area, where they are greeted with plastic flowers and cheers of "Welcome, welcome." People dance in the streets, waving rifles and defaced posters. Tongues are suddenly unleashed. Shiites pack into the al-Mokhsin Mosque, which has been closed ever since Saddam's agents murdered their much-beloved imam three years ago. Sheikh Amar al-Musadawi told the rapt audience that Saddam Hussein had betrayed Islam. He spoke of thirty years of oppression. He urged Muslims to save the country, not loot and destroy it. He said nothing about the Americans passing by outside.

Amer is wracked with conflicting emotions. "What happened to the Republican Guard?" he wonders. Though a Sunni himself, he says Saddam sealed his doom by refusing to allow Shiites into the Republican Guard, but included only Sunni Muslims largely drawn from his hometown and tribe. Amer lashes out at Saddam for fostering a hollow army rife with corruption and unable to defend the country. Bitterness bubbles to the surface as he speaks of the humiliation and worse that Iraqis have suffered at the hands of arrogant Republican Guards. He calls them puffed-up bastards who were good at throwing their weight around but couldn't fight like real men when the time came.

It's become evident from all he has said to me, and how he deals with people, that Amer has risen above divisions of tribe and Muslim sect to be first and foremost an Iraqi, and as I've watched him navigate this society, he has a way about him that makes him warmly received by all. He gives people dignity, and they return his respect in kind. And that also goes for the way he deals with me. I doubt he's ever worked for a woman before, but I get the feeling that as long as I am fair and straight it's not an issue. If anything, he's voiced sadness that men and women in Iraq still don't have the freedom to associate, to get to know one another, as he and I have done in these strange times.

Exhausted, we grab fried chicken from a take-out place. I am sitting in Amer's room about to chow down when we hear a commotion out the window. The Marines have finally approached the Palestine. I run down to witness their arrival.

I am stunned at how many Marines are packed into one Bradley. One after another emerges from its depths to take up guard duty around the hotel. Given the lawlessness in the city, it is reassuring to know they are here. Too many people, among them our former keepers, must know how much cash and equipment we have, and I had feared we would be a tempting target for thieves.

As more and more tanks lumber forward to the hotel, crowds begin to gather in nearby Firdos Square. A fifty-four-year-old taxi driver tosses his shoes at a statue of Saddam, a deeply insulting gesture in the Arab world. "We were surrounded by fear," he tells me. "Even fathers and sons were afraid to speak openly to each other." He recalls a friend who was arrested in 1978 and never seen again. "Thank you, America," he says, "for removing this dictator." He then joins a small group that tries to pull down the statue. After attempts with ropes and sledgehammers fail, the Marines move in a tank with a long boom to assist. The statue folds, falling to its knees, as the regime has.

The street scenes are nothing like as joyous as the cameras make them out to be. There are plenty of people standing around, numb or shocked at the events. Dr. Sa'ad Jawad, an Iraqi political scientist, watches sadly as the Marines help topple Saddam's statue, calling the scene humiliating. No fan of Saddam, he nonetheless warns of wounded pride. He acknowledges that now the Americans are here, they must be in full control, but he says their control will quickly be resented.

When I get back upstairs, Amer confesses that he wept as he watched the scene below. Though he too hated Saddam, he says seeing American troops in Baghdad is more than he can bear. He doesn't want their help.

Pulling down statues makes for good television, but as I saw in Moscow in 1991, it doesn't ultimately signify much. It doesn't begin to answer the deeper questions. Wiping out the past doesn't mean coming to terms with it. That's what Amer is struggling with: who are the Iraqis? How did they get a Saddam? How did they tolerate the fear Saddam created? And where do they go from here?

At dusk a group of men sits outside their shuttered shops, hoping their presence will deter the growing number of looters. They too are in shock at the sudden collapse of the regime. "I've never known freedom," thirty-three-year-old Ali al-Abadi says, the tremor in his voice revealing a jumble of mixed emotions. "We want a just government, but we want a just Iraqi government," he adds. Asked if they can name Iraqis they would like to lead them now, these men all shake their heads. That's the problem, they say. The Iraqi opposition in exile which has been courted by the United States inspires no confidence. Each of them just wants power for himself, they agree. They want nothing to do with anyone who has just come back from living in luxury abroad while they themselves have suffered at home. And they all fear paroxysms of revenge as past scores are settled.

BRENDA BULLETIN: APRIL 9, 2003

Annie called early this a.m. Baghdad is again more or less quiet after the drama of yesterday. She was adamant in her belief that the scenes of wild welcome that filled our screens were restricted to almost "made-for-TV" demonstrations. I get the feeling seven of the eleven people seen dragging Saddam's bronze head down the street were TV cameramen. One event, however, was very real. When the U.S. Marine tank column emerged out of the gloom yesterday morning, our ambivalent war-weary wench wept.

The eeriness of the vacuum at the hotel yesterday was pervasive throughout the city. Suddenly, by some mysterious stroke, all the security thugs who had turned the Palestine into a holding pen were gone. However, in the hours before midnight, Uday al-Tae did the rounds, playing on residual fears. Annie and her mates figured that he must have collected about $200,000 in pocketed cash. In an odd incident, he slapped and assaulted the Al Jazeera rep—a political ally in all this—when the latter presumably objected to the amount of the expected tribute.

Annie was worried about Amer and spent much of the day with him. Like many Russians she had known, who had trouble dealing with the loss of Stalin and what that said about their own destroyed lives, Amer was far from jubilant. Quite the opposite, she found him deeply depressed because they, the Iraqis, could not effect the change themselves. Despite his personal bond with Annie, despite his clear understanding of how despicable the regime was, the sight of Baghdad filled with American troops was, for this proud and decent man, a very sad day.

Now that the thugs are gone, the Palestine is filling up with grimy ex-embedded journalists and a small detachment of U.S. military. And there is also a growing number of "arrivistes," the just-drove-in-from-Jordan crowd in their crisp foreign-correspondent-multipocketed-Orvis-fishing-vests, complaining about the rigors of their journey. Somehow, I think their reception from the dirty denizens of the Palestine wasn't quite what they had hoped it might be. It just isn't Annie's crowd anymore.

Later in the day she encountered a strapping young Marine Corps officer in the Palestine. They approached each other in a manner that you can imagine to be perhaps the penultimate scene of an HBO special. Stopping six feet away from her, he says, "Ma'am, I wouldn't come any closer. I haven't had a shower in quite a while." "Funny," she replies, "I was going to say the same thing to you."

Lastly, there was that wonderfully absurd message from the Coalition High Command, wherever they are, following the shelling of the Palestine: "Hang sheets out your windows so that it won't happen again," they suggested helpfully, to which those in the Palestine replied, "Just who the fuck do you think has sheets?"

V

APRIL 10, 2003

I wake up to hear the creak of tanks moving their positions. My view today includes a contingent of Marines guarding the Palestine Hotel. When I come down to breakfast, or what passes for it, dozens of young Marines with their weapons slung over their shoulders, and still wearing their flak jackets, have already inhaled the food. It's hard to believe they found the stale bread and hard-boiled eggs tempting, but it must make a change from MREs, and sitting at a table sure beats boiling coffee on top of your tank.

After more than a month on the road, these kids are desperate for some soda—better still, beer—and a young officer asks me if I know where he can buy some Bacardi rum. I have to give him the bad news that the liquor stores are still locked, including Tiger Eye, which had once promised to do "good business" when the troops arrived. I offer him the bottle of gin from my private stock, but filthy as he may be he has his standards, and he stubbornly holds out for Bacardi until he is persuaded that it's gin or nothing. I reassure him it's all the same color and throw in a case of Cheer-Up for his unit, who are now guarding the Palestine roof.

I catch Amer looking at all these young marines with a mixture of bewilderment and wariness. The hotel management was scared by their arrival but, now more at ease, they offer officers a place to take a shower, even if only a cold one. The Marines have now set up roadblocks around the hotel and are checking everyone, including us. Security has its drawbacks, and what strikes us all as just a little bizarre is that our passports aren't valid ID. They want to see the yellow cards that were issued by the enemy Iraqi government.

Under Saddam's strict regime, Iraqis have all had to carry IDs which quickly reveal if they are government employees and which branch of the government they work for. They also indicate if someone is active military or in the reserves. Amer pulls his out. It shows he is a civilian who fulfilled his required reserve duty. Many Iraqis who had the "wrong" jobs have torn up their cards, but the absence of an ID card just makes people more suspicious to troops manning the checkpoints, and they are taken aside for questioning.

The looting continues. While some Iraqis wave white handkerchiefs overhead to cheer the American military on and protect themselves, others continue to plunder government offices. Today, it's turned into a family affair. Women and children have joined the crowds, helping to lug away whatever they can find. Lamps, chairs, and fans are particularly prized items. At Mustansarieh University a professor watches, helpless, as everything including the light fixtures are removed. He begs me to call in the Marines to protect Iraq's intellectual future.

An Army detachment has been searching the Al-Rashid Hotel, and Eric Westervelt, my NPR colleague, is with them. It's still not safe for me to get over to that part of the city. The staff at my former home has disappeared. I wonder what's happened to Faez and Mohammed, who took such good care of me.

A company of Army engineers goes through the Al-Rashid room by room to check for snipers and booby-traps. They blow up locked doors in the basement and the first floor and then they destroy the mosaic of George Bush I, over which I walked so many times. They try to remove it in one piece, but in the end they have to chip it out bit by bit. So much for dreams of auctioning it off on eBay. But even when the tiles are gone, Eric tells me on the phone, there's still an imprint of Bush's face in the floor. His memory here is not so easily removed.

Despite the scenes of celebration widely broadcast back in the States, the city seems somber to me. Iraqis are afraid of anarchy. They are afraid of themselves as much as they are of the Americans. And while most now admit to being glad Saddam may be gone, they are at best suspicious of American intentions and influence. Educated Iraqis warn again and again in interviews that we should not be deluded by the signs of welcome.

Amer and I drive into al-Adhamiya. Many who live here are Sunni Muslims, and al-Adhamiya has been home to many Baath Party loyalists. Yesterday we heard that Saddam had stopped at a mosque here, where he was applauded by supporters. He then disappeared. Today the mosque has been turned into an armory. Inadvertently, we come on a firefight. Iraqi Fedayeen and Arab volunteers are shooting it out with American troops. The fighters move through the narrow streets, using the mosque as a rocket-launching pad and the civilian houses for cover.

A car is burning ahead of us. We pull to a halt next to a house when a family, cowering in a walled courtyard, calls to us. A woman pokes her head out the gate, crying in English, "My husband, my husband!" She points down the road and we see him lying in a doorway a block ahead of us. He's been shot. He had run out to save a neighbor, whose car is the one smoldering in the distance. The residents plead with us to save the man in the car as well as his would-be rescuer. No one could possibly be alive in the charred car, and it's much too dangerous to venture close to it, despite the TV signs pasted on our windows. In a split second we decide to inch forward toward the wounded man. We jump out of the car, each of us grabs an arm, and we throw him into the backseat.

I don't do any of the things I had been taught as an EMT. I don't check airway, breathing, or circulation. I don't protect his spine. We just haul him out of danger and get him back to the family house, where everyone starts screaming. Amer carries him in. The young children sob in terror as their father is laid out on the floor in the main room. He has a shattered ankle. We offer to take him to a hospital, but the family says they will take care of things now. As Amer and I wash away the blood he looks at me with a smile and says with a certain amount of surprise, "You are very brave." I look at his suit, now covered in blood, and tell him the same.

People up and down the street continue to hide from fighters, some of whom, during a lull, tell us they are Syrians and Algerians. Clinging to its last moments of power, the Baath Party warned people there would be a fight, and it's been going on now for several hours. Abdel Majid Ahmed, who quickly identifies himself as a sixty-two-year-old customs official, is sheltering in his courtyard, which provides little protection from the surrounding gunfire. He says he still lives in a world governed by fear. "We have been in a big prison," he whispers, "and we are still afraid to tell all we want. It's terror."

We speed out of this battle zone and drive to a complex that has inspired perhaps the most terror, the General Security Directorate, one of the buildings Iraqis wouldn't dare look at when they passed it. Even now, with the Marines in residence, Amer approaches gingerly.

The Marine guards say I can't enter because I am not an embedded reporter, and they have nothing but disdain for Amer. I hit the roof. Finally though, after much to-ing and fro-ing, a very young public-affairs officer appears and I'm let in. New to Baghdad, he doesn't fully understand what this complex means to Iraqis. It has been badly damaged and was abandoned just before the bombing began on March 20 because the security apparatus knew it was a target. Marines, combing the fifteen or so different buildings, have found no prisoners. Nobody knows what happened to them. What they have found is a well-equipped hospital. Saddam's henchmen certainly looked after their own. Twenty-two-year-old Corporal John Holworth says corpsmen have recovered what they estimate to be more than a million dollars' worth of pharmaceuticals, which they plan to redistribute. They have also found a movie theater. The taste in films ran to action flicks like the Rambo series. One entitled *Amazon Women* sparks some interest among the Marines, but an officer says somewhat wistfully that there isn't any porn.

Like the Nazis and the Soviets, Saddam's Baathists kept copious records of their sins. Large quantities of documents had been shredded before the personnel fled, but Marine intelligence officers say there are still thousands upon thousands of dossiers that they haven't had time to go through. Many appear to include denunciations by neighbors or co-workers. This doesn't surprise people outside, who say Saddam's network of agents had turned Iraq into a nation of snitches. Paid informants would betray people for as little as $10. Sometimes, they say, lives would be destroyed just because of personal grudges or malice. When I go back outside, crowds begin to gather around the car. People have been frightened to approach the Marines, but they are not intimidated by our TV signs. Car after car pulls up next to us, their drivers demanding to know if the Marines have found any prisoners. Their faces fall when I tell them no one has been located inside. They can't believe it, insisting I tell the Marines there are underground cells they might not know about. Everyone seems to have a friend or relative who disappeared. Forty-six-year-old Mohammed Abbas, a businessman, is looking for his brother, who was arrested twenty-three years ago when Saddam first came to power. The family has never heard from him again.

This was the gateway to Saddam's gulag, the place where Amer and I had seen the families of political prisoners gathered outside on the first day we worked together. They got no answers then, and today the Marines cannot help.

Iraqis are coming up to the American troops offering information, much of it so far about arms caches ("cashays," as the Marines call them) dotted around the city. A Marine lieutenant colonel gives me a tour of one of the smaller finds inside a nondescript one-story building in a riverside park not far from the Palestine. There are machine guns, dozens of brand-new AK-47s, mortars, and boxes and boxes of ammunition. Some crates are labeled in Arabic, some in English, some in Cyrillic. Some are labeled JORDAN ARMED FORCES. "This is nothing," he says. "We've confiscated truckloads of guns. I've seen a room literally filled to the top with mortars, mortar rounds, and ammo. You could stock a whole batallion, maybe even a division with the stuff." He said the problem for the Iraqis certainly wasn't a lack of weapons.

APRIL 11, 2003

Most of the looters are friendly, if unapologetic, saying, "We've earned this." But Baghdad remains a dangerous place and the looting is spreading. Some journalists have been roughed up pretty badly and in some cases have had all their money and equipment stolen. Amer retrieves my cash, which I gave him for safekeeping while it seemed possible that the security goons might relieve me of it. Given the hotel sweeps, he had hidden it in his car. This now seems like a stupid idea, since cars are being stolen left and right. He also pulls out a Kalashnikov and a revolver from the trunk. He had left me in blissful ignorance about the weapons, but now hands me the pistol and ammunition clips to keep in my handbag. He says we may need it on the streets. I take the gun. It's the first time I have ever held a revolver. It's heavier than I expected. Amer is puzzled at how ill at ease I am, and by my evident distress. I tell Amer I don't want it in the car, and that we need to get rid of the weapons right away. I don't believe journalists should carry weapons. By the end of the day they are gone, which is just as well as the Marines are now searching cars.

We do a palace tour, stopping first at the elegantly appointed mansion belonging to one of Saddam's daughters. With the exception of the carved wooden wall panels and the inlaid marble floors, there's nothing left. Not a stick of furniture, not even the light switches. Iraqis continue to flood in and gawk at what they had paid so dearly for. Many are appalled by the looting, saying it is against Islam.

U.S. troops have occupied the Republican Palace compound, so what hasn't been bombed is more or less intact, and it is tacky, a Babylonian version of Louis XIV's Versailles, complete with fake French furniture and gold-plated faucets. In what appears to be Saddam's bedroom there are racks of Italian suits, many with their tailor's labels still attached. In a side building there are hoards of luxury items—champagne, cartons of imported cigarettes, and Persian carpets, the sort of thing Saddam dispensed to his favorites. The gaudy villa once used by Saddam's son Uday and now largely gutted by a cruise missile hints at a lavish and lascivious lifestyle. There are paintings of half-naked women and photographs of unidentified men with their hands on women's breasts. Soldiers from the 3rd Infantry Division are merrily feeding antelope and sheep to the scrawny lions and cheetahs they have found in what was his private zoo.

The home of Saddam's infamous cousin Hassan al-Majid has been stripped bare by looters, who emerge with scuba gear, water skis, and a complete kitchen still in its boxes. The same goes for the house of Tariq Aziz. By the time I get there, about the only things left are a book by Richard Nixon and a set of novels by Mario Puzo. These tours do little to answer who these men really were.

Many Iraqis are increasingly upset at the U.S. military's inability or unwillingness to stop the looting, which has now escalated to arson. Government ministries are on fire all over the city. It's by no means clear who is setting the fires, or why. It is quite possible this is not simply looting, but that remnants of the old regime are using the confusion to destroy records. In any event, people are worried that, as there is nothing left to steal in government buildings, looters will move on to private stores and houses, which so far have been largely untouched.

A lieutenant colonel in the Marines says the military has taken the city much faster than civilian planners back in Washington had expected. He defends the Marines, saying, "We aren't trained to be policemen," and quite apart from not wanting to get involved in "police business," he says fighting is still going on and the Marines don't have the extra manpower to stop the looting. But soldiers with the Army, who actually are trained to do police work, are equally dismissive of the prospect of peace-keeping, one saying bluntly, "I'm a trigger puller." It does seem that the U.S. administration is pitifully unprepared for the task of protecting the people they have conquered. Even after Bosnia, Kosovo, and Afghanistan, the young soldiers on the ground don't grasp that they are here to keep peace as much as wage war.

The overall lawlessness raises the specter of revenge killings. Some journalists watched as a Baath Party official ran toward American troops for protection. He was being pursued by a group of young men determined to kill him. It seems this official had made a handsome living by turning in army deserters for a bounty. One of his victims pulled up his shirt to show the scars from his arrest at the hands of this particular official, who he says shot him and hurt many more people as well. The official managed to escape, but I suspect his days are numbered.

A convoy of journalists has arrived at the Palestine today from Amman, and they're being joined by dozens of dis-embedded reporters. It's the end of an era in more ways than one. Our intimate war, with no networks and no stars, has turned into the usual gang-bang. When I see Dan Rather and Christiane Amanpour wandering down my floor, I realize it will soon be time for me to leave. I can't help but feel, "What are they doing in MY hotel?" I find myself feeling raw and exposed in the midst of this new crowd.

It's scant consolation, but our yellow ID cards, the last to be issued by the Information Ministry, have become a badge of honor of sorts, a sign that we were here through it all. You can also tell us by our dirty clothes. I call Loren and tell him I've got a week's worth of work left in me.

BRENDA BULLETIN: APRIL 11, 2003

If the Palestine Hotel ever did, in fact, resemble the set for a grimy adaptation of *Henry V*—"Once more unto the briefing of Baghdad Bob, dear friends, once more"—it does no longer. Closer to the mark would be a milling mob scene from *Ben-Hur*. The place is seething. Three hundred journalists have arrived, people crammed three and four to a single, the staff nonexistent save the fellow collecting money, power and water still out, the food even worse.

Annie got some sleep but still sounds tired, and she has a cold coming on. She has a few things to wrap up, including finding better quarters for the incoming NPR group.

She doesn't buy the notion that for a while a good chunk of this country hung on her every word out of Baghdad: "Anyway, in two weeks everyone will be on to something else," is her dismissal. Perhaps, but if only as something of a public service I want to close with a précis of some of the hundreds of letters that NPR has received and forwarded to me. Her editor firmly announced he could paper a room with them.

What was mentioned over and over was just the quality of her voice that made many an NPR listener sit up early, instantly aware, or put a hold on breakfast, or pull the car off the road, or drive around the parking lot until she was finished, or just simply stop what they were doing. Many mentioned that tone of hers, that low husky veracity she gets in her voice when she has something important to say. She delivers it, softly enunciated and understated, nuance expressed often in the spaces between the words. Whatever she was, tired, weary, scared, appalled, it came across in the inflection if not in the words themselves. People woke up early to make sure that she was all right.

There's one letter that particularly got to me. This writer adopted Annie as her "trusted war correspondent" and described her voice in the morning as becoming "familiar, comforting, almost like sharing a ride with a friend." She talked of Annie painting a picture so clearly that "I feel I am looking out her window with her. I have smiled as she described the ridiculous ironies of war, and have driven my car with tears streaming down my face." The writer signs the letter "Your car-pool buddy."

Cheers to all.

V

APRIL 12, 2003

The American troops are still doing little to stop the looting, and Iraqis are furious that one of the first and only buildings the United States has protected is the Oil Ministry. This will not easily be forgotten and reinforces what many Iraqis fear: that the United States is here for oil and only oil.

The military have opened traffic over two bridges that were blocked by incinerated cars with charred bodies inside. Looters are now able to move into areas that had so far been untouched. At the Planning Ministry, looters forage for furniture and computers with American troops standing nearby. The Al-Rashid Hotel, which the military left unguarded after they checked it out yesterday, has now been trashed.

Iraqi professionals—engineers, teachers, doctors, and police—converge on the Palestine, demanding that the United States reestablish order and electricity so people can get back to work. Harried civilian-affairs officers try to respond but are overwhelmed. Many who have turned up were fired by Saddam's government years ago and are seeking both justice and their old jobs.

It's going to be a complicated business sorting out who's who, and nowhere is this clearer than in the lobby of the Palestine, where poseurs and wannabe Iraqi politicians hold impromptu press conferences, jockeying for the attention of the international press. Each claims the honor of having been at the top of Saddam's Most-Wanted list. Many, dressed in ill-fitting camouflage, have come in with the American troops. Though they are distinguished by the initials FIF (Free Iraqi Forces) on their sleeves, their quasi-military attire has many confused about who they really are and they deliberately play on this. They reinforce the misguided impression that they actually have some authority by making grandiose promises about how they will get the water and electricity back up in no time. I can't help but think that these people could be doing something more useful than generating hot air. While they mouth off, Shiite clerics are working at the grass roots, organizing neighborhood-watch groups and medical assistance. And the competition for power is undoubtedly going to be followed by a grab for the Baath Party's real estate. I can see a replay of what happened when the Soviet Union fell apart and the wiliest, and not the wisest, got their hands on former Communist Party property.

A Marine checkpoint keeps most other Iraqis out of the hotel. The young soldiers are nervous about suicide bombers after an attack last night, and they are simply not prepared for the onslaught of distressed, confused people. Many of those crowding around the gate have come to plead with reporters to let them use their satellite phones, now the only operating phones in the country, so that they can tell relatives abroad they are OK. I stuff my pockets with notes from several people, promising to e-mail their families.

In the crowd I see Saleh, my last, sweet, useless minder. His family survived, though the Rashid military base next to his house was pounded again and again as expected. My less-than-sweet former minder Sa'ad also turns up. He takes one look at me and darts in the opposite direction. Undoubtedly he is not advertising his years with the Information Ministry and he is right to fear I will make sure any newly arrived, innocent journalists are aware of his background. Mohammed, the head of room service at the Al-Rashid, also appears, looking for work. Having left the Al-Rashid unprotected and open to looters, the U.S. military is now planning to take up residence in the damaged premises but, suspicious of former employees, doesn't plan to rehire them. In Mohammed's case they are making a big mistake. I tell him I will help find him work with one of the news organizations. Majed, my former driver, also arrives desperate for employment. He is deliriously happy that the Americans are here, even though his house was damaged yet again in the bombing. He gives me a big, scratchy, unshaven kiss.

Lorenzo Cremonesi of *Corriere della Sera* has emerged from his netherworld to work legitimately again at last, as has John Burns, who need no longer fear the knock in the middle of the night. Mark Ubanks, the human shield, can meet his cutoff day of April 15. Larita Smith is still wandering around and I pass on messages from her family, who contacted me after the story about her aired. I don't tell her that none of the reports she sent out reached her Jackson, Mississippi, TV station. We weren't taken hostage. Our satellite phones weren't fried by fancy U.S. weapons. The battle for Baghdad collapsed before it really started.

With the war basically over, Amer's Japanese contingent has also returned. I tell him NPR would love to hire him on a permanent basis. I think he might stay with us if I were to continue on, but I tell him I will be going home for a break soon. He has a contract with the Japanese that he feels bound to honor and says he has to think about it.

APRIL 13, 2003

I don't have a week left in me after all. The bubble has burst. As much as I want to cover the immediate aftermath, I am wiped out. Jackie Northam, another reporter from NPR, has arrived, and I realize I need to get out for a while, but there are a few things left that I still need to do to close this chapter.

At the al-Kindi hospital, which I've visited so many times in the past, twenty-six-year-old Ahmed is one of the few doctors who's so far dared to come back. He's manning the emergency room alone, but he spares time to talk. He says there are maybe enough drugs for another two days but he has no way to sterilize anything. He points to a patient lying over to one side. He has just put in sutures with no sterilization.

There's still no electricity. The bodies in the morgue are rotting because the refrigerators don't work and relatives haven't been able to come to pick them up. The number of newly wounded has dramatically decreased, but Dr. Ahmed is seeing many patients with old wounds that are badly infected because they couldn't get treatment. All he can do for now is give them antibiotics and tell them to return when he's got more help.

As the medical staff trickles back they are relieved to see that the damage from looting isn't as bad as rumored or as they anticipated. The hospital's medical college has been gutted, many windows are smashed, and stretchers and wheelchairs litter the courtyard where looters were stopped before they could wheel them away. The most valuable equipment is safe, though "No thanks to the Americans," a doctor snaps into my microphone.

The first to protect the hospital were armed volunteers who came from a mosque in the poor Shiite neighborhood of Saddam City. Now they are working alongside Marines, who've at last taken up positions outside the hospital. Sergeant Tylan Wilder says the Iraqis love them, but it's not that simple. There is tension between the Marines, the Shiite clerics, and the medical staff who worry that the clerics are aiming to take over the hospital. Future power plays are already looming.

Sheikh Abbas al-Zuwaidi, a thirty-year-old Muslim cleric, admits he is at best ambivalent about the American presence. He's grateful that Saddam has been overthrown, but as he looks at the Marines, he declares, "They are against Islam." For now, he's taking a pragmatic approach, saying the priority is to help people. And while suspicious of the Marines, he has even tougher words for Arabs in other countries who supported Saddam.

Sheikh al-Zuwaidi and many of the volunteers working with him are former political and religious prisoners. Al-Zuwaidi is a follower of Mohammed al-Sadr, the spiritual father of the Islamic Dawa Party which was founded in 1968. Like the Ayatollah Khomeini in Iran, al-Sadr called for an Islamic revolution. He was executed by Saddam. Al-Zuwaidi was lucky; he was merely detained and tortured for forty-five days. He lifts his robe to show the scars from beatings and electric shocks. He says he was left to crawl back to his cell, pulling himself on his hands and elbows. Doctors assigned to the prison refused to treat him unless he paid them. Two years later, his knee is still bandaged.

At Baghdad's Neurological Hospital, there's only one doctor in attendance for the thirty remaining patients. Dr. Anwar Hafel has no idea how many patients have died for lack of treatment in recent days, and there's no way yet to figure out overall military and civilian casualties. U.S. troops now stationed down the block from the hospital have given him a whistle to blow if looters should attack, but he says that's not enough, explaining, "We want a government now to help with electricity and water." He says it's more dangerous now than it ever was during the bombing.

I am still trying to figure out what happened in the market bombings, the two incidents that claimed the most civilian lives.

Dr. Hafel treated the victims, and he says he is sure the Iraqis, not the Americans, were to blame. He says the injuries were not consistent with an American bomb or missile. A military officer as well as a doctor, he says he knows weapons, and he knows what kind of fragments he removed from the victims. He blames the attacks on errant Iraqi SAM missiles and antiaircraft chaff.

We also stop at Al Jarrah, a small private hospital where a lack of supplies and electricity could soon be compounded by looting if the United States doesn't do more. Dr. Azzidin is one of the countless Iraqis who believe Americans should have been better prepared for what has now happened. If there was a lack of justice under Saddam, he says, there is now an absolute security vacuum, which was utterly predictable. He is exhausted and scared, and his eyes well up with tears. He's a professor of gynecology at Baghdad's medical school. It's been pillaged and burned.

As we move from hospital to hospital, a young Marine screams out, "Hey, weren't you the lady on the bridge the other day?" I confess I was. He confesses he nearly killed me. It's a small world, sometimes frighteningly so, and I can't help but recall another similar incident in another place at another time.

Back in 1998, I was standing on another bridge, which marked the dividing line between the former Soviet republic of Georgia and the breakaway territory of Abkhazia. I was trying to persuade a so-called Russian peacekeeper to let me pass. He would have none of it, but asked, "Haven't I seen you two somewhere before?" I was with an NPR colleague, Michael Sullivan. I answered that I thought it highly unlikely since we had never been in that particular part of the world. He then proceeded to describe in graphic detail what Michael and I had been doing hundreds of miles away in the Chechen capital of Grozny a year before on Easter Sunday. His description of our foray into the Russian Orthodox Cemetery was chilling in its accuracy. And where, I asked, were you? "On a roof looking at you through my gun sight," he replied.

Perhaps I have been doing this too long.

APRIL 14, 2003

Secretary of State Colin Powell says the United States will play a leading role in the effort to recover or restore antiquities that have been looted from Iraq's national museum, but it's a little late. In the months before the war, scholars repeatedly urged the U.S. Defense Department to protect Iraq's priceless achaeological treasures. When it came time, the military says the museum fell between the operational areas of two battalions. They say there were no specific orders from above to guard it.

Still in shock, Iraqi curators have yet to begin documenting what has been stolen or destroyed. Museum guards say they stood by helplessly as hundreds of looters, many of them armed, broke in. They took sledgehammers to locked glass display cases. They broke into vaults, where some of the most valuable items had been hidden. In their wake they left a trail of trashed offices, ransacked galleries, and bitterness. Dr. Dorry George, director of research and studies for Iraq's State Board of Antiquities and Heritage, says people from the museum have repeatedly begged the American troops to help, but that they still have not appeared.

I had been told before the war that many of the most valuable items were removed for safekeeping, and despite reports that "everything" is gone, Dorry admits he is not sure what was saved and what wasn't, but he lists some of the museum's most cherished items, which he asserts *have* been stolen: 5,000-year-old tablets bearing some of the first known writing, a 10,000-year-old pebble with twelve scratches on it, which is the first known calendar, and the 5,000-year-old Sacred Vase of Waurka, which shows a procession entering a temple and is the earliest known depiction of a ritual anywhere.

Iraq is the home of ancient Mesopotamia, often called the cradle of civilization, and Iraqi pride rests on a cultural heritage that goes back thousands of years, but three days of looting has eliminated what had survived invasions and wars in the past. While many of the looters may have come from impoverished districts of the city, others seem to have known exactly what they were looking for. Dr. George picks up some glass-cutters lying on the floor, noting that this is not the usual tool carried by a looter. The fact that the offices and museum records were systematically destroyed is also disturbing. All this raises questions about a possible inside job, but George won't contemplate this. And while he says Iraqis may have done this, he says they did it with the tacit blessing of American troops. But others who have come to survey the damage can't believe it was Iraqis who looted their own heritage. If not Iraqis, then who? I ask. "I don't know," answers one curator. "Jews," says another. Iraqis are going to have trouble accepting responsibility for much of what has happened, not just in the past few days but over the past thirty years.

The National Library, another repository of Iraqi history, has also been ransacked and burned, the reading rooms and stacks reduced to blackened rubble. Tens of thousands of ancient manuscripts, books, and newspapers documenting Iraq's history from its zenith a millennium ago through the turbulent Ottoman rule to Saddam Hussein are nothing but ash.

As we drive back to the hotel, we maneuver through sections of Baghdad where residents have set up obstacle courses of tires, rocks, and furniture. Clusters of men, old and young, stand guard with Kalashnikovs and chains, ready to beat off anyone who dares to loot. Anyone passing by with stolen goods weighing down the car is stopped and forced to give them up. Amer is relieved to see that people are beginning to take responsibility for their lives and property.

While I write up my last broadcast, Amer comes up to the room. He sits quietly while I send the report, the first time he has actually seen what I do. He nods in approval at my descriptions of chaos and confusion. He refuses a glass of "medicine." He wants to talk, and says he needs a clear head. "I was not a school-teacher as I once told you," he begins. I am somehow not at all surprised, but I wonder what is coming next.

He tells me he was once an officer in the Iraqi army. He looks for my reaction. Relieved that I don't appear shocked or appalled, he continues. He attended the military academy and served in the Iran-Iraq war and then in southern Iraq during the Gulf War. He says proudly that he was a good officer who was loved by his men. He had a promising career, but in 1995, pre-cisely because of his abilities and his position, he was ap-proached by "The Tikritis," shorthand for members of Saddam's inner circle. They wanted him to help with their illegal traffick-ing and proposed he act as a courier. They courted him. Amer says he refused, not once but several times. For this he was stripped of his commission and demoted from captain to a foot soldier in Saddam's reserves. Deliberately humiliated, he was lucky to get away with his life.

It all suddenly makes sense: his bearing, his taste for suits that he wore like a uniform while others wore jeans, his dignity, his sense of honor and responsibility, his pride in his "professional-ism," his confidence that he could protect me, his exact knowl-edge of things military, his fury at how Saddam had corrupted and destroyed the military and the country. He is still at heart an officer, and as he talks I can hear his pain and profound sense of loss. But I have to ask what I have never dared before. Was he working for Iraqi intelligence all along? I want to hear him say no. He does, but then he turns the question on me. "Who are you, really?" He needs to hear that I was not working for the CIA, though he admits he had become convinced of my "innocence" when he handed me the revolver back in the car and saw I was clearly out of my element. He then tells me how close I was to being detained over the past weeks, how he deflected charges that I was a spy. I believe what he says.

We talk well into the night. We hurtle from subject to subject, reliving events, gossiping, and then grappling with what it means that my government has conquered his country. We try to grasp this moment, unwilling to let go. What is unspoken is that we have come to love each other. We've seen each other in the most intimate situations imaginable, instants of fear, exhaustion, bravery, and trust. Our backgrounds are so different, and our futures so different, that at times we have to pause, to try to explain the unexplainable. I ask him if he wants to be an officer again, in a new Iraq. He can't answer.

I promise I will be back before long. I tell him I will bring him to the United States for a visit, but he says it's too late for him to think about going overseas. Iraq is his home and his destiny. As I have come to know all too well, helping Amer is not easy. With twenty-two-year-old Mimosa, who did so much for me in Kosovo, I was able to help arrange graduate school in the United States, and become a kind of surrogate mother. Irina, who ushered me through the fall of the Soviet Union and the rise of a new Russia, has become a sister. What has been especially rewarding about these assignments is the sense that I have somehow been able to repay the people who have helped me, if only in small ways. That helps bring some measure of resolution to situations that are not easily resolved. But I don't know what I can ever do for Amer. Perhaps I will be able to do something for his children. He is family.

APRIL 15, 2003

The convoy of GMCs prepares to leave for Jordan. I've got a seat. I wake Amer up one last time with "our knock." He comes downstairs to the lobby. We don't talk, and with the phones out and e-mail cut, I don't know when we will be able to again. Finally I hug him and we both start to cry. I climb into the car, and I look back as the convoy pulls out of the Palestine. We wave.

The trip out is uneventful. There are burned-out Iraqi vehicles along the way, and only one American checkpoint where soldiers wave us through. There are no Iraqi border controls. The buildings have been destroyed, along with the life-size portrait of Saddam I had studied for many an hour while I waited to be processed in the past. This time there are no bribes, and no wrangling over the AIDS test.

When I get to the hotel in Amman, I turn on the shower and stand in the streaming, steaming water and find myself sobbing uncontrollably. I have left part of me behind in Baghdad, an intense, cherished relationship that can never be recaptured. The story is far from finished. But I want to go home. I want to see Vint. I want to thank him for understanding. I call to say I am on my way.

BRENDA BULLETIN: APRIL 18, 2003

Down a weight class and sniffly, Annie wheeled into JFK late yesterday unsure if the bombing of Baghdad was any worse than the thirteen-hour BA flight from Amman. Voluble for the first seventy-five miles and at a cheeseburger stop, she drifted off and fell silent for the last bit. But she was only preparing for her first-night-home routine of nudging furniture back into place and of cuddling all living things in this ménage that needs only a bare light bulb to be a *tableau vivant* of a Booth cartoon.

She came home to a house full of flowers, strawberries and clotted cream, a box of lotions and skin unguents, champagne and Kit Kats, an offer from some California River Guides to take her down the wild river of her choice, and a hotel in Washington suggesting a free dirty weekend.

Out of her kit came only two small mementos of Baghdad: a string of glass chandelier beads found on the floor of one of the palaces, and a small fringed flag bearing the words "Iraqi Shooting Federation" (Saddam's son Uday was its benefactor). Out, too, came the unread collection of Montaigne's essays, the unembroidered pillowcases, and the unused Kevlar codpiece.

A number of weeks ago, a good and most literate friend sent me the perfect line with which to close this chapter of the Brenda Bulletins. Until last night, I could not utter the words aloud lest the ending be jinxed. But now, with great joy, I can. Scheherazade, that other fabulous female storyteller of Baghdad, ends the saga of *The Thousand and One Nights* with the line, "And then it was morning."

Indeed it is. Happy Easter to all,

V

AFTER

Days go by and I cannot contact Amer, and he cannot contact me. Finally I receive an e-mail slugged "Medicine":

Dearest Annie,

This is Amer from Iraq. Don't be surprised regarding this e-mail because I am now in the north of Iraq where there is Internet access. I hope it works and you receive my message. I miss you. You take a big part of me when you leave.

I want to tell you that I can't live with this new situation. Don't doubt my feelings about the past regime, but I start to feel people have changed for the worse. It is very dangerous. I have lost my bearings and I don't know how to deal with people.

Attention: you cannot reply to this message because I will return to Baghdad in a couple of days.

I hope to see you as soon as possible.

Best regards, with high consideration,
I remain,
Amer

MAY 10, 2003

A few days later Amer manages to use a satellite phone to make a call. It's frustratingly short, but I am deeply relieved to hear his voice again. He continues to work for the Japanese, so employment is not a problem, but the overall situation has not improved. He is still groping for hope. More than a month after entering Baghdad, the United States has yet to restore electricity or impose order. Thieves have taken over the streets. Aid organizations cannot operate because of threats, and it is unclear which Iraqis will rise to the top in this chaos.

The reasons I stayed have been justified and ignored in ways I had not anticipated. It turns out that Iraqis precisely predicted what would happen, and though many of us working in Baghdad had long reported what Iraqis thought and feared, the Bush administration has apparently heeded little of it. So accurate from the air, its initial reaction to events on the ground has been slow and inept. Iraq is a complicated place, rife with contradictions and divisions that the Iraqis are the first to acknowledge. I hope the United States employs the wits, wisdom, and patience to do what it can to ensure that this war doesn't spawn another.

And then there is the question of the weapons of mass destruction, which the United States swore it knew all about, and which supposedly justified this invasion. After more than a month of U.S. occupation, they are yet to be discovered. Could it be that Saddam was actually telling the truth when he said they had all been destroyed?

Though President Bush has declared that the war is over, American troops continue to face resistance from former Baath Party loyalists, Islamic fundamentalists, and unemployed Iraqis, including former officers. Fired, these officers feel betrayed by the occupying forces to whom they effectively surrendered as requested. Iraqis are not persuaded by the President's declarations that they are now free, and the administration appears reluctant to invest the troops, skills, and money to help rebuild the kind of Iraq it says it wants.

Iraqis, American soldiers, and journalists continue to perish. A close friend, Elizabeth Neuffer of *The Boston Globe*, survived the worst of Bosnia and Rwanda to die when the car she was traveling in hit a guardrail on the way from Tikrit to Baghdad. She was fearless in covering war crimes and human rights abuses, and she had returned to Iraq to report on the aftermath. I have lost many friends before, but her death has left me reeling. We met after 9/11 in Pakistan and were delighted to "find" each other. We were close in age and remarkably similar in appearance, and we had a similar take on the world and how we wanted to write about it. No shrinking violet, our Elizabeth was someone I could spar with, laugh with, and shop with. I imagined working with her in Baghdad in the coming months, perhaps years, and I looked forward to getting old with her. I have lost another part of myself in Iraq.

ACKNOWLEDGMENTS

The trip to Baghdad started almost thirty years ago when I became a correspondent for ABC News. That rash and fateful assignment was made by Av Westin, who dared to believe I could do it. At National Public Radio there were people who once again dared to let me follow my instincts: Kevin Klose, Bruce Drake, Barbara Rehm, Loren Jenkins, and Doug Roberts. I can't begin to say how much I relied on their support and their verbal hugs, which even the sat phone could not distort. My thanks to everyone at NPR, a place where I dearly love to work, as well as to the listeners whose letters of concern, encouragement, and healthy criticism made me realize more than ever that this is a remarkable radio family.

Over the years I have been gone from home more than most families should or would tolerate, but I have an incomparable husband, two glorious stepdaughters, Gabrielle and Rebecca, and an absurdly large extended family who have put up with it all with stubborn love and infinite patience. Teeny and Warren Zimmermann and Pie and Alfred Friendly, who were responsible for this marriage, and hence for my sanity, picked up the slack when I disappeared, and they welcomed me when I returned. The Wednesday Group, John Funt, Kenneth Maxwell, and Christopher and Betsy Little, provided sustenance in more ways than one. And Vint's harem, Chris Stansell, Dorothy Wickenden, Elizabeth Becker, and Ann Cooper, called regularly to check in on him and the dogs, making sure I had a husband to come back to.

Editors do make a difference. Jonathan Galassi immediately saw what this book could be, and with but the gentlest of prodding, the most incisive of comments, and Sunday-morning conferences, got this non-book-writer to do the impossible and finish on time.

Thanks to friends, family, and colleagues in many countries, but a special toast to those who were with me in Baghdad.